I0004671

One Data – Achieving business outcomes through data

Disclaimer
The material in this publication is of a general nature only, and does not represent professional advice. Whilst every effort has been made to make this book as complete and accurate as possible, no warranty or fitness is implied. The author disclaims all responsibility and liability to any person or entity with respect to any loss or damages arising from the use of information contained in this book.

Every attempt has been made to cite quotes and other referenced material. The author acknowledges all third party trademarks and copyrights, and the use of a term in this book should not be regarded as affecting the validity of any trademark.

The reader should be aware that referenced Internet resources and articles might become unavailable at any time.

BPMN symbols reproduced with permission from Trisotech Inc. For a free 30-day trial of the Trisotech BPMN modeler visit www.trisotech.com

Publishing Information

First Edition: May 2015

ISBN-13: 9781511722476 (ebook)

www.shanedowney.net

Contents

List of Figures

List of Tables

ACKNOWLEDGMENTS

Writing this book has been some twenty years in the making, and is my way of giving something back to the industry that I have enjoyed so much.

I have been very fortunate to work alongside some amazing people – every interaction is an opportunity to learn and I thank them for sharing their knowledge with me. In particular, I owe a debt of gratitude to Tanya Brock whose experience with managing and implementing large projects has helped shape some of my thinking; particularly in the area of change and adoption, and Chris Lawler for her thoughts and ideas on dialogue, flow and suggested material.

I would also like to acknowledge the contribution from Denis Gagné, CEO of Trisotech, for allowing the use of the Trisotech BPMN modeling tool.

To my family – my wife Michelle and my four boys Connor, Hayden, Jared and Liam who have taught me the value of knowing, and whom I have taught the value of storytelling.

To my late Mother, Ursula, for always believing in me, and my late Father, Jim, who once said to me "you need to get a real job – these computers aren't going to get you anywhere". I would also like to express my appreciation to current and former employers and clients; organisations who have taken me on and empowered me to be part of some truly exceptional projects.

Finally, to all the *Data Minions* out there (you know who you are) – my personal thanks for your support and your contribution.

Dedicated to the memory of my good friend and colleague Jen Tang.

HOW TO USE THIS BOOK

"Here is Edward Bear, coming downstairs now, bump, bump, bump, on the back of his head, behind Christopher Robin. It is, as far as he knows, the only way of coming downstairs, but sometimes he feels that there really is another way, if only he could stop bumping for a moment and think of it. And then he feels that perhaps there isn't."

— A.A. Milne, Winnie-the-Pooh

Sound familiar? Do you ever find yourself feeling as though you're continually "banging your head" and not making any real progress? This book will help you identify the real problem and present a strategy for delivering real outcomes.

A few years ago I was in a meeting with a group of around twenty stakeholders. A new statutory reporting requirement was looming, and a meeting had been organised to ascertain what, if any, impact there might be. I was simply there as an invited guest so I was just there to listen. The meeting organiser explained the problem (i.e. this new reporting requirement), and then individual stakeholders were asked how it might impact their system. It became very evident that almost every system would be impacted – the scale of the impact was significant. On conclusion of the meeting I was asked if I had any ideas on how this problem could be solved. That became the catalyst for this book – to answer the question "Where do I begin?"

I have always been a fan of repeatable processes (i.e. patterns) as a way of solving problems; figure out how to do something once and then refine, adapt and reuse. This book is designed to bring together a number of approaches into a single template for data centric projects. It explores some of the many tools, technologies and frameworks that are available and incorporates both standards for information management and best practices.

I've taken some of the best bits of what I've learned over the past 20 years or so and combined them into a pattern for One Data.

This book is split into three parts:

Part I: The Principles of Information & Data Management
For those of you who are new to information management, this part of the book will provide you with some of the knowledge you will need to lead a successful outcome. If you are already an information management practitioner then you may want to skip this part (although hopefully you will find some useful insight).

Part II: One Data
These chapters describe the One Data pattern in detail.

Part III: Leadership & Communication
To be successful in any project activity, good leadership and communication is paramount. These chapters provide some handy tips that can help take your vision through to a successful outcome. You can have the shiniest new solution but if the users aren't engaged then you've failed.

What isn't covered in this book is how to develop software as there are a multitude of books and resources available plus formalised education courses. This book does discuss the various options and considerations for procuring a solution.

I hope you find this book useful and wish you the very best of luck in your journey.

INTRODUCTION

"Begin with the end in mind."

- Stephen Covey

What are data centric projects?

Historically organisations have been predominantly driven by process and workflows. Since the Industrial Revolution, organisations have been using advancements in machinery in order to increase production speeds and reduce costs (mostly related to wages and labor). The introduction of computers enabled the development of much more sophisticated automation – just look at any modern factory. The other outcome of the use of computers was the removal of vast amounts of paper records and the introduction of the electronic storage of information, triggering the Information Age. I believe we are now in an Information Revolution; the availability and affordability of smart devices and the Internet means we are more globally connected than ever before. Organisations can no longer rely on traditional processes and work flows, they rely on information – complete, accurate and as timely as possible so as to be able to make key decisions quickly and maintain or establish a competitive advantage.

The traditional way that software engineering is taught begins with requirement gathering, then design and build of the screens, design and build the database, and then design and develop any reports or data extracts or data integration interfaces. I call this functional design and development. The focus is on the core user functions; often based in what the functions are that people currently perform in their role.

The problem I see with functional design and development is that not as much thought and consideration is given to the data. The database design is frequently a byproduct of the development cycle, reporting is often an afterthought, and interactions with any other system are often picked up during development resulting in data integration "spaghetti" which become a support nightmare.

Recently, I was asked to provide a data extract out of an in-house developed application. My standard response to these sort of request is "Sure – but is there an existing application report that you can use?" In this case, the response I received was "There are no reports – we didn't think we would need them when we built the system." All systems are designed to provide an outcome and there is always output as a result of that activity, so it comes as a surprise anytime people believe reporting, extracts or data integration are not required.

A data centric approach attempts to consider all of the data requirements of the system first and then design and build application functionality to manage the data. The resulting system may require business processes to change but you will have a richer and more streamlined application.

My approach to data centric projects is to begin with the end. Start by considering what the desired business outcomes are. Is there a problem that needs to be fixed, or a short-term or long-term strategic goal to be achieved? By understanding the problem and the vision, you can begin to dig deeper into your solution requirements.

Next, consider what information will be required as output from this system for internal and external consumption. You need to consider reporting, data extracts and data analytics. Systems are designed to produce output so you will get a better outcome if you have a solid understanding of what output is required.

Identify what your sources of data are. What is the information flow? What is the quality of the information? What data has to be manually entered? What data feeds (interfaces) already exist?

Finally, how does all the source data align with the output requirements? Are there any gaps? If so - where will you source this data from to fill the gaps? This will also help flesh out any calculations required, and any data transformations required to make the data suitable for consumption.

Now that you have a detailed understanding of your data domain, you can design and build robust database structures and processes. You can also design and develop any data warehousing requirements for data analytics purposes.

Once the database and related processes have been designed, you can develop the application components to manage the data, reports, extracts and interfaces, along with any other functional and non-functional requirements.

The final step is change and adoption - reviewing the existing business processes and looking at how they may need to change in order to support the new system. Change and adoption may require additional (or fewer) people, and may require people to be retrained. This needs to be managed in conjunction with any Human Resource requirements. Ideally, areas that are likely to require change are flagged during the design phases.

There is no business decision that can be made without information. By focusing on the data you will generate better and more useful information that can enable better business decisions.

The remaining chapters will look at the One Data pattern in more detail.

PART I: PRINCIPLES OF INFORMATION & DATA MANAGEMENT

"Data is not information, information is not knowledge, knowledge is not understanding, understanding is not wisdom."

- Clifford Stoll

In order to have a successful data centric project you must first have a good understanding of the principles of information and knowledge. This chapter discusses these topics in detail.

CHAPTER 1: INFORMATION AS KNOWLEDGE

Knowledge comes from applied learning. Every time you take something that you've learned, apply it, and then assess the outcome, you're generating knowledge. When you take the knowledge and apply it to other situations then that becomes wisdom and learning.

Imagine if you could align all of your core data assets, transform the data into meaningful information, and then apply that information together with the knowledge of your employees in order to reduce costs, increase sales, or improve your product or service offering. This is the value of knowledge management.

Organisations seek to achieve their strategic and operational goals by channeling the collective knowledge of the employees in a unified direction.

The pyramid of wisdom

The pyramid of wisdom (otherwise known as the DIKW pyramid) represents how through continual improvement, refinement and reuse of data we can achieve great things.

Figure 1 - The DIKW Pyramid

Data

Data (or datum) relates to the specific (sometimes referred to as atomic) values. Data is often referred to as the *facts* – discreet results of one or more function or process. Your first name, family name, and date of birth are all very commonly used data items as a means of identification.

Data represents the gathering of factual information, especially information organised for analysis or used to reason or make decisions. In computer terms, it is represented by structural numerical and textual or other information represented in a form suitable for processing by computer.

Because data is the result of one or more processes, it must be *"right"*.

Data is always right. If it doesn't look right, check the processes right back to the source.

A dataset is a logically related group of data items. For example, information about a person (name, address, telephone) is often referred to as Demographics. When you bring together related datasets you establish Master Data.

Master Data Management is the process of managing Master Data and covers identification, retention, access and security, reporting, and governance.

Lately you will have been bombarded with emails, blogs, articles, and vendors all talking about Big Data. Big Data is nothing particularly new – just an acknowledgment that the volume of data being produced and consumed globally is increasing at a fantastic rate.

Information

According to founder and data management expert John Owens of John Owens International, *"data has no intrinsic value"*. I've always believed that data has no meaning without context; without understanding how it came to be, how it is structured and how it is used. John continues, *"data that doesn't relate to business functions is waste"*. I believe that, if you understand the business you're in, you may identify information that may be useful in the future – and often it's easier to capture that information earlier than later. The tradeoff though is how much potentially useless data is captured in your systems. Without context it is difficult to determine what present or future value the data might have.

Information is the collection of related data that is processed, analysed, organised, classified or communicated in order to serve a useful purpose, present facts or represent knowledge. Information brings context and meaning to data.

Information = data + context.

Knowledge

When you take information and make use of it, you learn more about it. When you take information from multiple sources and combine them, you gain a deeper insight into the processes that created the information. These learning's are the foundation of knowledge.

Knowledge = Information + Learning's.

Wisdom

If knowledge is the learning achieved through the use of information, then wisdom is the application of those learning's in order to better model, analyse, and predict business outcomes.

Wisdom = Knowledge + Applied Learning's.

Information management

Wikipedia defines Information Management as:
"...the collection and management of information from one or more sources and the distribution of that information to one or more audiences. This sometimes involves those who have a stake in, or a right to that information. Management means the organisation of and control over the structure, processing and delivery of information."

Sources of information include paper, computer systems and electronic devices. Audiences can include computer systems, reporting and analytics.

Successful organisations understand the value of their information and use it for effective decision-making. Understanding the value of information means establishing robust governance practices, data stewardship, and the ethical use of information.

Information management is all about managing risk. Your organisation's information is your second biggest asset (beside your people) and must be treated just like any item of value. Risk is managed through governance and information management does this through establishing the boundaries; values and principles that will determine the appropriate management and use of data, and these are endorsed by Executive Management approved policies. Information governance is covered in more detail later in this chapter.

Information & data governance

We've briefly touched on the information management function of governance of data and managing risk. But what is governance? According to the DataGovernance.com website,

"... a system of decision rights and accountabilities for information-related processes, executed according to agreed-upon models which describe who can take what actions with what information, and when, under what circumstances, using what methods."

Good information governance requires you begin with a strategy covering the following subject areas:

	Key Elements of a Data Governance Strategy
i.	Definitions/Glossary
ii.	Policies/Procedures
iii.	Stakeholders/Interested parties
iv.	Committees/Working parties
v.	Key Performance Indicators
vi.	Privacy and Ethical use
vii.	Data Security

Table 1 – Key elements of a Data Governance Strategy

Definitions/Glossary

It is crucial that everyone understands the terms and references used in conversations and documentation. Is *spaghetti* a kind of pasta or a plastic sheath used to insulate wires? (It's actually both!) It depends on the context of the customer. The best way to achieve this is to create a Glossary of terms that contains key words or phrases and a short definition. This should be a living document that everyone has access to read and the definitions must be agreed upon by the organisation. The project team should own and maintain the document.

There may be industry specific glossaries available on the Internet to get you started– you just need to look!

Policies/Procedures

A Policy is a document that states the acceptable management of a specific risk.

Stakeholders/Interested parties

Stakeholders are senior members of the organisation who are key decision makers. These are the people that you will want to make understand the problem and seek their buy-in when presenting a solution.

Committees/Working parties

Governance cannot be undertaken in isolation. Bringing together the stakeholders is required in order to make any significant progress. These are the people who will make decisions.

Key performance indicators

KPIs are part of the Balanced Scorecard method for monitoring outcomes and this methodology can be used to monitor any activity. KPIs can be used during a project to ensure the project remains on track, and can also be used to monitor business as usual activities as part of continual improvement.

Privacy and ethical use

Managing data means ensuring that it is only used for the purpose in which it was intended. This is the basic premise behind meaningful use. Your organisation, local or federal Government may have regulations that govern privacy and ethical use, and you need to establish policies that enforce these regulations including the penalties for breaches of policy.

Data security

Information security is a very broad and challenging subject area. Essentially it answers the question of how will you ensure privacy and ethical use. Information security requires policies around the secure storage, retention, use and destruction of information.

Information architecture

Information architecture is part of the Enterprise Architecture discipline, and is the mechanism by which information needs are determined and appropriate models, frameworks and classifications established. Or more formally:

"Information architecture is the means by which information is structured and categorised, including the technical and application technology in use, and the business rules and governance in place to support it, in order to facilitate business growth"

The value of information architecture is documenting the current state architecture, so as to facilitate safe technology change through being able to provide advice and knowledge to future information technology projects.

Information architecture is an implementation of information management governance. Information architecture takes the governance model established by the information management function, and establishes the execution model. For example, a common data management principle is "data should be encrypted before being shared with external organisations" – but how do you make that happen? That's the role of the information architect – to take that principle and come up with a concrete mechanism to implement it.

Chapter summary

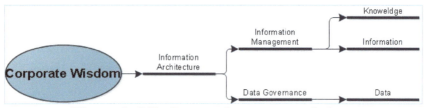

Figure 2- Mind map of corporate wisdom

This chapter explored the concepts behind establishing corproate wisdom which enables information project delivery. Corporate wisdom can be achieved through the use of information architecture. Information architecture is comprised of two facets – information management and data governance.

Data management is the discipline of understanding holistically all of the key sources of information, where and how they are produced and consumed, and identifying the value to the business and the organisation in general. Information management requires a governance framework incporproating strong policies and procedures in order to effecitvely and efficiently manage information.

Data governance is the discipine of taking the frameworks, models and decisions outlined in data management polices and procedures and ensuring they asre implemented across all datasets. Data governance includes identifying tools and technologies to assist in ensuring that the data lifecycle is robust and reliable and the data is fit for purpose.

CHAPTER 2: DATA MANAGEMENT

Data management is the discipline of managing enterprise data as a corporate asset. DAMA International describes data management as:

"The development, execution and supervision of plans, policies, programs and practices that control, protect, deliver and enhance the value of data and information assets."

We've already discussed the governance aspects of information management. The remainder of this chapter discusses the programs and practices that are essential elements of information management.

Data lifecycle management

Paper-based Record Management systems of the past identified that data flows through the following stages:

	Data Lifecycle
i.	Capture/Produce
ii.	Cleanse/Transform

iii.	Distribute/Consume
iv.	Store/Maintain
v.	Extract/Report
vi.	Archive/Delete

Table 2 – Stages of the Data Lifecycle

Capture/Produce

This is in relation to the source of the data; where it is created or produced. Traditionally, the source of data is paper with Data Entry operators manually typing the data into fields in a computer system. Increasingly, other sources include electronic devices such as sensors and counters, and electronic document management systems where paper documents are digitally scanned and stored in a data repository.

It is during this process of capturing or producing data that it can be catalogued giving the data context. For example, if the data has been written onto a form, then you know what the type of form is, what the captured fields are, and how that form is processed. You can also determine what data is "required" vs. what is "optional".

Cleanse/Transform

Rarely is data immediately fit for the purpose of sharing. Formats for data such as dates and money often require adjusting, and value ranges may need validation to ensure that only acceptable values are shared.

Cleansing and transforming data is a step that may projects either don't do upfront (and discover the hard way later), or they don't put enough effort into it and so only pick up a few of the more obvious pieces and typically these are just the tip of the iceberg. As the Titanic discovered, it's the stuff beneath the water that you can't see that will bring your project undone!

Distribute/Consume

Once entered into a computer system, the information is immediately available for use. Typical use includes search and display. More advanced consumption involves the sharing or distribution of data to other computer systems. See the section on Data Integration for more detail.

Store/Maintain

Data must be stored in order for it to be retained – typically in a data repository (or database). Once stored, the data can be maintained (added, amended, deleted) via data entry screens.

Extract/Report

A lot of data will end up extracted either as a spreadsheet or in some printed report, typically for the purposes of historical reporting, or historical data analysis. Typically, the data being analysed is old enough that it doesn't change much. This kind of analysis is somewhat useful in that it enables you to see *what happened* – but it doesn't necessarily tell you *what is happening* – or *what will happen*.

Archive/Delete

Storing data over time typically consumes an amount of storage space and this can become costly. In addition, the more information in a computer system the longer it takes for a search operation to complete. Computer systems often provide a maintenance archive function that will take information older than a specified timeframe and move it onto another storage medium. Sometimes, computer systems offer a delete operation however; this should be used with caution, as in most cases once deleted the information can never be recovered.

Depending on your organisation and state or federal legislation there may be very specific requirements around archive and delete operations.

Data stewardship

I have experienced conversations in which people argue over "who owns the data". The answer is data is owned by the organisation and everyone who interacts with corporate data is a custodian. As a custodian, we're all charged with the responsibility of properly managing the data just like any other corporate asset.

Pragmatically though, you need to have people who are solely responsible for the day-to-day management of the data asset. This is the role of the Data Steward. Ideally, the Data Steward is the subject matter expert and knows how the data is created, where it is consumed, and is aware of, and manages, data quality issues in the source system.

Just a note of caution when dealing with software vendors. I have encountered vendors who believe that they own the data and therefore attempt to restrict/prevent access to it (particularly if you choose to move away from their product). The vendor owns the intellectual property relating to the structure of the database only. They cannot own the data content. To minimise any legal wrangling over data, ensure that your contract with them stipulates that – should the contract with the vendor be terminated by either party, that the data is made available to you in a format that can be generically read (such as structured text files or XML files).

Data structures

Data exists in three primary forms – structured, semi-structured, and unstructured.

Structured data

Structured data is highly organised, categorised and specific. Data in a spreadsheet would typically be structured data. Structured data conforms to a known set of rules.

Semi-structured data

Semi-structured data is less organised, and yet still conforms to rules, however the rules tend to be less well defined as structured data.

Unstructured data

Unstructured data doesn't conform to any rules, and therefore is open to interpretation. The content of an email, or a video clip are examples of unstructured data.

Computer systems are designed around structured data because it is the easiest to work with. Unstructured data is the most complex to work with because programming a computer to somehow find some meaning inside the data is challenging. Social media (i.e. Facebook, LinkedIn, Twitter, etc.) are all examples of unstructured data, yet by examining the posts and likes from people you can gain incredible insight into what people think of your products and services.

Below is an example of structured, semi-structured and unstructured data in the form of basic customer demographic data.

Figure 3 - Structured vs. semi-structured vs. unstructured data

Let's suppose you want to run a marketing campaign. You have a new product and you'd like to inform your customers about it. You've designed a flyer and you're ready to send it – you just need a list of postal addresses to send to. If your customer data is stored in a computer system or spreadsheet then you have a starting point. If you look at the previous figure, you can identify in the structured and semi-structured data that they are addresses. It doesn't tell you if the address is home, postal, work or some other address – but at least you have something tangible to use. Consider though if your address information is stored in a more generic (or what we call "free text") field. The content of that field could contain anything – not even address related. So before you can use that data you first have to profile it (data profiling is discussed later in this chapter) in order to determine what entries represent usable addresses, what entries contain an address but other information that would need to be stripped off, and what entries are entirely useless. Once this activity has been completed, you can then consider using the data for mailing your flyer. If you have 100 entries then this profiling and cleaning exercise wouldn't take long. What if you had 1,000 addresses, or 100,000 addresses? It's the scale that becomes the biggest issue.

Unstructured data is largely an untapped resource within most Organisations – purely because of the complexity in making sense of it. There are languages and dictionary tools available that can help scan (or parse) free text looking for keywords and phrases. For these tools to be effective they require highly configured language syntax and dictionary vocabularies that are specific to the nature of the data. For example, there are tools that can take an unstructured set of Doctor's progress notes for a patient, extract the principle diagnosis and treatments, and standardise the resulting data using standardised health vocabularies.

The risk of using unstructured data is that the input is largely unrestricted and therefore open for people to enter whatever content they like. Without the context of the data, unstructured data lends itself to misinterpretation.

Static, reference and transactional data

These are characteristics of data and the way it is produced. It is very important to understand these characteristics with data that you're working with as getting it wrong can impact your data quality. There's nothing worse than when you have built your system and business processes around core data only to discover that it isn't behaving the way you had expected.

Static

Static data never changes from the moment it is created. Unique identifiers for records and control values are typically static data. Be wary of making assumptions about static data without fully investigating where the data is produced, how it is used within processes and what happens to it when the process is finished with it. Date of Birth (as registered with a statuary births register) is a reliable source and could be deemed accurate. But someone stating their date of birth may have chosen to take a few years off their age. Social Security numbers can also change depending on which Country you're in. In Australia, when a baby is born it is allocated the same Medicare Number as the Mother. But once the child turns 16 years of age he or she can obtain his or her own card, which will have a different number.

Reference

Referential data is used primarily as a technique to reduce the amount duplication of common data items. For example, instead of storing the name or description of a product every time it is purchased, you create a code-value pair – e.g. "P12345" = "Widget". The code would typically be a static value, and the name and description could change over time, however they are only stored once. All references to that product use the code "P12345". It is very common to have the database designed in such a way that there is only ever one code-value pairing table an all codes and values are stored there.

So a date of birth as obtained from a registry office would be considered static data, but a Medicare Number would be considered reference data in Australia.

Transaction

Transactional data is the result of one or more activities. A line item in a purchase invoice is a good example. Also think about your own personal banking. If you read your bank statement it contains a list of transactions.

In database terms, a transaction is also a way of grouping one or more activities into a single event. One of the biggest problems in database systems is when an operation requires multiple database updates and some work and some don't. You end up with this hideous mess where you don't actually know what the state is. For example, imagine if you had a process that called a banking system to debit a customer account and that failed but your application thinks that it was successful and so marks the purchase order as paid. You've just lost revenue. But if you encapsulate the process in a database transaction and the call fails then the transaction is automatically cancelled and no data is saved which means there is no revenue loss.

Data quality

The term *data quality* is the generalisation of a broad subject area. Data quality refers to the data being complete, accurate, timely, and fit for purpose. The quality of the data (when broken down as above) can be measured quantitatively and monitored in order to ensure a level of confidence in the processes that produce it. More advanced Organisations will have trigger points or thresholds related to the monitoring of quality aspects and will raise alerts when those thresholds aren't met.

Governance is a key component of data quality using proactive measures to prevent poor quality data. Often organisations confuse data correction as being data quality. Fixing data errors is waste and a result of poor data quality governance.

Complete and accurate are self-explanatory.
Timely data refers to the data being available whenever it is required.

Fit for purpose is a little more interesting. Data should not be used for a purpose other than, for which it was created. Data itself is meaningless without context. If data is used out of context then the values are not only meaningless but are likely to have an adverse effect. For example, just because a particular product sells well in one country doesn't automatically mean it will sell just as well in a different country. Data and context (otherwise known as *Metadata*) is covered later in this book.

Data Quality = the right data, at the right place, at the right time.

Data profiling

Professional trackers of animals or trespassers such as poachers look for clues in their surrounds. Known as spoor, these clues are the footprints, impressions in sand or mud, broken twigs, compressed grass – anything that, when combined, one can draw a reasonable conclusion as to the direction the target went.

Data profiling is much the same – it's the practice of data analysis; of looking for clues in the form of patterns in data. How do you know your customer email addresses are valid? How do you know that values in a column in a database are valid? Data profiling assists in understanding your data through establishing rules. You can do this visually but using a data profiling tool allows much more powerful (not to mention faster) analysis.

By implementing rules, you can quickly identify exceptions in your data. For example, if you apply the standard format for an email address to the data in the database for customer email addresses it will highlight any email addresses that are improperly formatted.

Data profiling can also help link data in different data sources. By examining patterns in the data, data profiling tools can identify not only potentially matching data columns but also match the data within those columns. An example of where this would be useful is in examining address data that might be stored in your Customer database with address data stored in your Billing database.

Another benefit of data profiling is identifying unused data that might be of use. Through data profiling, you gain great insight into your data, where it comes from, and how it is used. Data profiling can also help bring meaning to *Dark Data* – which is covered later in this book.

Metadata

You may not recognise the term *metadata* – but you interact with it constantly. Metadata is literally *data that describes data*. The easiest way to identify the difference between data and metadata is to look at some examples.

If you have the value "61799999999" what does it represent? Is it a bank account number? Is it a social security number? Without context, it's meaningless. But if I told you the value was actually a telephone number with the first 2 digits as the Country Code, followed by a single digit which is the Area Code, and then you have the information (i.e. the metadata) that you need to decode the value. In this case, "61" is the Country Code for Australia, and "7" is the Area Code for Brisbane. The remaining digits are the actual telephone number. Taking that example further, because you know that the first 2 digits are the Country Code, we can establish a business rule that says "all Country Codes must be between 1 and 999". So the number "012799999999" would fail that business rule check. This is how you ensure data accuracy.

Another example is date formatting. Every country has its own way of representing a date. Take the date "10/12/2014". Is that – the "10th December 2014?" or the "12th October 2014?" Without knowing either the format the date was recorded in or the locality where the data was captured, it's impossible to tell. But if I told you the date format is "DD/MM/YYYY" where "DD" represents 2 digits for the day of the month, "MM" represents 2 digits that are the month of the year, and "YYYY" represents the 4 digits for the year, then you know the date as the "12th October 2014". The date format pattern is the metadata in this case.

Metadata is also housed in the way the data is stored. Storing "10/12/2014" in a field called "next_appointment_datetime" with a data type of "Date" provides a clue that the data value is the date of the next appointment. Similarly storing "24995.00" in a field called "product_price" with a data type of "Money" provides valuable insight into what the data value means and how it should be used.

To be able to take full advantage of Business Intelligence we must capture not only the data value but also as much metadata as possible. That way whenever we interact with the date field, we know how to properly format it for display, or how to include the value in a search.

Dark data

"Thar's gold in them thar hills!"

I'm a huge fan of the various *"Gold Rush"* type shows that frequent on the Discovery Chanel. Seeing how, even with modern technology, just how hard it is to get gold out of the ground; it's no wonder gold is so valuable!

Hidden deep inside your organisation lays secret data. It's produced and consumed within business units. It's not categorised, it's not readily accessible outside of the business unit, and the business unit is heavily dependent on it. It typically exists in desktop spreadsheets, little home-brew databases, or proprietary applications. All too frequently, a former employee built the spreadsheet or database and nobody else has the proficiency to modify the programs, or knows where the program source code is, so support is always an issue. Very rarely is the data backed up making fault recovery nearly impossible. Sound familiar?

Dark data is a relatively new concept yet it could be an absolute gold mine, but it is buried deep inside your organisation.

The only way to gain insight and access to dark data is to mine it, beginning by surveying your business. Identify areas producing an output and record your findings using the following elements:

Artifact Log
Artifact Name
Artifact Owner
Business Unit
Purpose
Technology in Use
Usage Frequency
Known Issues
Major Data Elements

Table 3 – Contents of an artifact log

Once the artifacts had been registered, the organisation was able to determine how to manage them based on a risk assessment. For example, high and medium risk artifacts can be better documented and perhaps marked for replacement with a better management system. The register should be published so as to create awareness.

Once you have a catalogue of dark data, you then have an opportunity to analyse and profile the data to identify any that would be useful to your organisation. Not all dark data will prove useful. It may be a missed opportunity due to poor data quality, or it may be a byproduct of the business function – you may not want this data in your data warehouse, but from an information architecture perspective, it may prove extremely useful in service analysis and redesign.

Data integration

Data integration represents an aspect of the Consumption phase of the Data Lifecycle. It is rare to find one software application that can perform all of the processing that an organisation needs. If you look at the typical structure of an organisation, each business unit will have software specific to their function. For example, the Human Resources department will have one or more HR and Payroll systems, while the Finance department will have accounting and billing systems. Both business units need to share information so how is this achieved? Historically, these areas relied heavily on paper records and the movement of paper records and manual processes. With computerised systems comes the opportunity to share electronically. Organisations with less mature use of information typically still print and share paper reports, creating inefficiencies around the double entry of data and the risk of poor data quality. Data integration resolves these issues by automating the sharing of information between computer systems.

Data Integration = Movement of data between computer systems

Real time vs. near time vs. batched

Real time data is data that can exist in one or more places simultaneously. The speed at which the data needs to travel is typically reserved for device driven data only. Electronic switches, signals, counters are all sources of real-time data. Biometric devices that are used to monitor specific aspects of one's health (such as heart rate, pulse, temperature, weight) are also sources of real-time data.

Near time data is data that exists in one or more places almost simultaneously. There's no real definition of "almost" but there is some notional delay (even if its sub-second) between when the data is produced at point A, and when it arrives at point B. The delay is usually because the data has to be read, packaged and then sent.

Both real-time and near-time data tends to be small, discreet parcels contained in a "payload" (a structured format surrounded by header and footer content). The focus on these parcels is speed over content, which is achieved through keeping the information as small as possible.

Batched data is data that is usually extracted as part of some process. Typically, batched data occurs on a regular schedule ranging from once a minute to once a day (or even once a week/month/year).

Depending on the frequency of execution, the amount of data moved is typically much larger than real and near time.

Message driven

The discreet parcels described in near and real time data integration are forms of messaging. Message driven architecture requires one or more producers and one or more consumers. Messages are produced by events – an activity or action within a system. For example, the sale of a product on an online shopping site might generate a sell message to a system responsible for distribution, and generate a message to trigger the transfer of funds from the buyer's credit card to the seller's bank account.

Push vs. pull

Message based integration usually follows a push model where the message is pushed from a source system to downstream consumers.

Batched data integration is typically a pull-push model; the data integration process connects to system A, and then extracts (i.e. pulls) the data required. After processing the data, the data integration process will then connect to system B and push relevant data to it.

Data integration via interface

An interface is the implementation of a data integration *"contract"* between the system producing the data and the systems that are required to consume it. Using properly designed interfaces enables data governance. If you prevent direct access to the data in systems and you make data available through interfaces, then you have control over exactly who has access and for the intended reason.

Data sovereignty

This applies to data being transferred across country boundaries or being hosted on data servers in other countries and must be a key consideration when you are looking at hosted "data in the cloud." Countries such as Australia, Singapore and the USA have strong governance around data privacy and security. Many other countries are far less rigorous. So when evaluating a hosted solution (even of the vendor is local to you) always verify exactly where your data will be geographically stored and then investigate what national data regulations are in place.

I worked with a local vendor once who hadn't completed their local data center and so we had to send test data to their data center in Canada. Unfortunately we didn't discover this until after the contracts were signed. The project ended up being delayed about two months until the local data center was completed.

Data in the cloud

It's hard to find an article these days that doesn't mention cloud computing. Essentially, cloud computing is an external service in which you typically pay a subscription for someone else to host and manage parts of your IT infrastructure. Otherwise known as managed, hosted, or out-sourced services, the concept of cloud computing isn't new.

The cost of tier-1 storage (fast disk) is expensive and the demand for storage is ever increasing. Storage is a bit like money – the more you have the more you use and therefore the more you need. The notion of data in the cloud is to say that instead of continuing to buy storage devices (and related infrastructure), and expanding data centers for the hardware to sit in, you buy storage on someone else's managed infrastructure and they manage your data storage for you. The main advantage of this model is scalability – in theory if you want more or less storage you just change your subscription.

As with a managed service, there are risks and so here is a list of questions you might like to consider asking when evaluating a vendor:

	Considerations for Data in the Cloud
i.	**What is your policy regarding vendor staff access to data?** - Vendor staff should have no access to data – just the devices that manage them.
ii.	**What mechanisms are in place to prevent unauthorised access to data?** - When considering this factor in your own staff, vendor staff/visitors, and external access from hackers.
iii.	**Where is the data physically stored – onsite, inter-state or overseas?** -Recall the discussion about data sovereignty. Depending on the sensitivity of your data you might not want it to be stored physically in certain lower security countries. You may even

have a policy or legislation that states the data can't leave your country.

iv. **What is your process for the backup and retrieval of data in case of emergency (i.e. there is a fire on site)**
- This is about ensuring that your data is considered to be an asset and treated as such. The vendor should have both onsite and regular offsite backup options available, with fast turnaround times for recovery.

v. **What is your strategy for ensuring business continuity in case your facility ceases to operate?**
- Your business relies on timely access to data. What would it mean to your business if you can't access your data for a day, a week or a month? You must ensure the vendor has an alternative data center that is on standby in case of emergency, and you need to know how long it will take for that data center to become active.

vi. **When the contractual agreement ends, how will we gain access to our data?**
- Despite what anybody tells you – your data belongs to your organisation. So when the contract ends, if you choose to engage someone else, or host internally again, you will need full access to all your data in a timely manner.

vii. **Have all your staff undergone a criminal history check?**
- This should go without saying that you need to ensure the vendor staff have no criminal past that could affect your business. You should also enquire if any of the management or staff have ever been bankrupt or insolvent. People under severe financial stress are more likely to undertake fraudulent or criminal activities.

viii.	**Can you please provide a recent report from an independent auditor?**
	- If the answer is anything but "yes" then beware!
ix.	**What is your level of compliance with standards such as ISO 27001?**
	- There may be other standards as well but not all equally apply in each country. If you're in the USA and you work in a healthcare environment then you might like to include the HIPAA Privacy Rule. Equally in Australia, new Privacy Laws were introduced in March 2014. If the vendor will be performing credit card transactions on your behalf then you should insist on them being PCI-DSS compliant.
x.	**How is the data stored – is it encrypted and where are the encryption and decryption keys kept?**
	- The easiest way to prevent anyone from looking at your data is to have it encrypted. But equally if something happens you need to know that the vendor has the keys to be able to regenerate your data! Ideally all keys (logins and passwords, encryption and decryption keys) should be stored physically in a vault.
xi.	**What support options are there?**
	- Your requirements will vary on this one depending on the nature of your organisation. If you operate 24 hours a day then you will require 24x7 support. But if you only operate during certain hours then you need less support. You need to understand the risk to your business and how long you can suffer an outage in peak and off-peak periods of demand vs. the cost of the support services available.

Table 4 - What to ask when evaluating a hosted service provider.

I would also recommend a site visit so that you can become familiar with the vendor's environment setup, security measures, and data center design.

Storing data in the cloud is a business decision and requires assistance from your IT department to make it all work seamlessly.

Remember – when you out-source your data or technology to an external party, you are essentially handing them the keys to your business so you have to be sure that every care is taken so that your business can continue to operate in all conditions and at all times of the day or night.

Open data

The notion of open data was formed around the concept of sharing data that can be used for the purposes of research. Open sharing of data could help healthcare research into illness and disease, causes, treatments and cures. For education, open sharing could help in constructing better education programs and learning techniques for improved learning outcomes. In the Government sector, open sharing could help provide better community services through a shared understanding of the socio-economic environment of the constituents and the locality where they live.

Open sharing of data will, in time, assist in the reduction of some of the costs, time and resources that go into research.

The challenge with sharing information between Organisations is there is no single standard way to package and transmit the data. Every system is different, and has different capabilities for the sharing of data. There are also regulatory restrictions around the appropriate use of data, and requirements for privacy and consent. These regulations may be different from one territory to another, and even more different between countries. Opendatahandbook.org is an excellent resource that covers this topic in greater detail.

Big data

The notion of data analytics (as discussed above) is nothing new. The concept of Big Data is part fact and part sales pitch in my opinion.

The premise (or rather – the promise) of Big Data analytics is the ability to not only unlock insight into your business but in doing so being able to predict the future and plan accordingly.

There's no rule that indicates you have a "big data problem". Rather, there is a set of descriptors that can indicate the magnitude of your data issues. These are commonly known as the *Five-V's*[1]:

	Five-V's
i.	Volume
ii.	Velocity
iii.	Variety
iv.	Veracity
v.	Value

Table 5 – The Five-V's of Big Data

Volume

Most small to medium size Organisations data volume are in the megabyte to gigabyte range. Data operations such as sorting, searching, reporting and editing tend to happen reasonably quickly using standard hardware and software.

A medium to large enterprise will usually have data in the terabyte range, which is still manageable with enterprise class hardware and software.

But large to very large enterprises that have a global footprint tend to have very large data volumes in the petabyte range. Performing analysis on this size data becomes problematic because even on enterprise class hardware and software, the time to analyse and process becomes lengthy

---

[1] Beware – vendors and service providers continue to invent their own "V" as a way to promote their products and services.

(days or even weeks), the data is too big to hold in memory and so the performance of the hardware infrastructure becomes an issue.

Velocity

Velocity is the speed to which new data is created. Data may be coming from devices including sensors, which can generate megabytes of data per minute. The challenge, when combined with the large volume of data, is how do you process data at that rate and size and be able to make reasonable quick decisions?

Variety

Data isn't just coming from single systems; it's coming from multiple systems and multiple devices simultaneously. In addition, the types of media have changed such that there are audio files, video files, images and photos. Then there are the semi-structured and unstructured data sources of Social Media; Facebook and Twitter posts that can provide incredible insight into customer sentiment.

Veracity

Veracity represents the speed and variety of data requests. Business leaders need up to date and comprehensive data in order to make smart business decisions. Organisations need this plus additional data in order to make decisions around products and services on offer. In a paper based world people are used to data taking months to be formatted and aggregated into something useful. When information is held in computer systems, people are expecting to be able to get access to meaningful data at least weekly. But the demand for information in order to undertake future planning requires meaningful information be available in near-time. Not only do we want as much data as possible - we want it now!

Value

As already mentioned the premise of Big Data is unlocking the secrets that are driving your business. This is the value proposition and is largely used by vendors as a means of demonstrating the return on investment for undertaking Big Data activities. If you're Big Data project is going to cost half-a-million-dollars then how do you sell that to your Organisations board? The answer lies in demonstrating the value that Big Data can bring.

The good thing is you can use the patterns in this book to deliver a Big Data project. The concepts are all the same it's just the scale that is different.

Business intelligence

Once you have a solid foundation for data analytics in place, how do you continue to get value from your investment? Business Intelligence (or BI as it is more commonly known) can help.

Data analytics tends to be backward looking by nature. Analysing data in order to see how many products were sold last quarter or how much profit was made last month. The problem with looking backward is it can be too late to identify and make changes to your business, and when you do make changes you have to wait another reporting cycle before you know if the benefits of the change have been realised.

BI is takes this historical data and applies predictive analytics techniques in an attempt to predict (or forecast) what the future might look like. This is a very agile way to run your business because as soon as you make a change you can see if the forecast models are predicting success, and if not then you have an opportunity to make minor adjustments along the way. BI empowers your business by answering questions like – am I on track to meet sales targets for this quarter?

The real power of BI lies in its dynamic nature. When leading a new issue of shares, Stock Brokers need to be able to not only identify clients who might be interested but also be able to identify clients who are actively trading at the time of the issue, as they would be the most interested. Looking at historical data would help identify potential investors by examining their holdings and value, but if they haven't actively traded in 12 months then they might not be so interested as opposed to someone who has made several trades this week.

One effective way to formalise a BI capability is through establishing a BI Centre of Excellence (COE), which combines data analytics with BI, reporting to an Executive Manager (commonly the Chief Financial Officer). A note of caution however, as these teams typically become not just the data analytics and BI team but also the reporting team, and the demand for reports can become overwhelming. A better approach is to have this team construct the underlying data structures and then empower the end-users to create and manage their own reports. This is where the data visualisation tools become very powerful.

In the old school days of advertising, a campaign would be established for a specific product or service. It would have a finite marketing campaign and so it is quite easy to determine if that campaign was successful or not simply by examining sales before, during and after the campaign against target.

But how do you identify an impact of sales of a particular product if someone posts a positive or negative comment about in on social media? What is the follow-on impact by people sharing or re-tweeting the comment?

According to Time.Com, the eye sight of a three-year-old child was saved by a photo shared on Facebook, after a friend (who happened to be a nurse) saw the clear reflection in one eye in the photo and suggested getting it examined by a pediatrician. The child was subsequently diagnosed with a rare medical condition. Imagine having the ability to search all photos or videos in sites such as Facebook in order to identify people who might have a medical condition. Clearly there is incredible value if this can be achieved so how would you make this a reality from a technology perspective and how would you manage the privacy and consent issues?

In April 2014, The Duke & Duchess of Cambridge visited New Zealand and Australia. According to The Daily Mail UK, the dress that the Duchess was photographed wearing sold out almost instantly. An information savvy business will identify these opportunities before time so as to ensure there is sufficient product available.

According to TheNextWeb.com, in August 2013, Chinese mobile phone manufacturer Xiaom released the first batch of 100,000 units of its latest mobile phone on the social networking site QZone. All 100,000 units were sold within 90 seconds of them being announced, and they have since racked up a staggering 7.45 million reservations by eager customers. If you are a product manufacturer and you don't use social media – you're already behind your competitors.

Empowering BI at the desktop is where the magic happens!

Data analytics

Data is everywhere in your organisation; it's the input and output from every business function, and making sense of all that data is a challenge.

Similarly, how do you know your business is performing well (or poorly)? If you want to streamline your business processes, how do you know where to look for problems that could be slowing you down? The answer lies in data analytics.

Data analytics involves taking data from disparate data sources and connecting that data to provide the big picture of what is happening within your organisation in order to make more effective business decisions. For example by combining product sale data with financial data you can see how much profit or loss has been made. If you add in customer data then you can also determine who are your biggest customers in terms of product purchases. If you add in manufacturing data then you can determine the cost of producing your products. All of this information can help you make better decisions around your product base and your customer base.

Data analytics is challenging and requires experienced people who know data. You also need good tools – tools that will help aggregate your data, tools that will help profile your data, and tools that will provide good analytics and reporting of your data.

Data analytics requires investment but it's an investment in the future of your business and one you simply can't afford to ignore if you want to establish and maintain a competitive edge.

Predictive data analytics

Data analytics uses historical data in order to plan for the future. The data in use could be days, weeks or even months or years old, and so it can be difficult to determine if a change of business process is yielding the desired outcome and the time to market on these changes can be quite poor as you adjust, wait for the next reporting period, check to see if you're on track, adjust again, and then wait until the next reporting cycle.

Predictive data analytics uses statistical modeling and mathematical techniques to attempt to identify patterns much sooner; effectively in real time and through visualisation techniques allows the business to see what is happening at any given moment in time. Some predictive models are able to "learn" and so improve their accuracy over time.

Consider the stock market. This is a highly volatile environment where changes in share prices can fluctuate many times per second. A stock broker needs to be able to not only monitor the real time market movements, but also be able to gauge what might occur next. Sophisticated trading systems use predictive modeling techniques to not only show the current market data, but help predict what might occur in the next 10 seconds or the next 10 days, giving the trader much finer management of their trades.

Financial institutions that provide credit cards use predictive modeling in order to identify potential theft and illegal use of fake or stolen credit cards to the point where the fraud detection system can automatically disable a credit card if the right conditions are met.

Hospital and healthcare providers use a variation of predictive analytics called clinical decision support. Clinical decision support systems use predictive modeling to identify when the health of a patient is deteriorating, or if a prescribed medication has the potential to cause harm because of an incompatibility with other prescribed medications.

If that doesn't give you a hunger for data (pun intended), CIO.com has reported that a particular pizza chain is using predictive analytics in order to determine what the level of success would be for specific kinds of promotions.

At present there is a significant amount of research and development in the field of predictive analytics and big data. Processing discreet packets of data quickly is a simple task, but processing large streams of data in real time and applying predictive modeling techniques is a bigger challenge due to the cost associated with the computer hardware and software required.

Data warehousing

A data warehouse (DW or sometimes referred to as an Enterprise Data Warehouse – EDW) is a collection of related data elements for the purpose of analysis and reporting. The DW includes both current and historical data in order to facilitate trending analysis and forecasting.

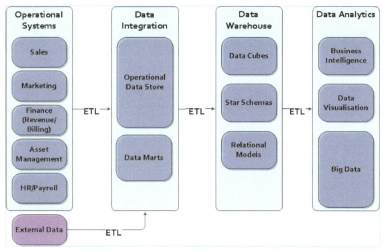

Figure 4 - Example of a data warehouse for product sales

In order for data to make it into the DW it usually passes through a three-stage process known as Extract-Transform-Load (or ETL).

Extract

The extract process identifies data in source system of interest. For example, customer data from the customer database, sales data from the product database, and financial data from the billing database. Automated processes are developed to extract the data on a regular (typically nightly but could be intra-day) basis.

Transform

Certain data elements will need to be adjusted in order for them to be usable. They might be coded values and your users will want to see a description on the report, or perhaps the data requires some cleaning.

These processes occur during the transform stage with the end goal being a set of data that is fit for purpose.

Load

The final process, the load process, is required to take the transformed data and load into the DW. Often the internal structure or model of the warehouse is different to that of the source systems and so the load processes have to take the data and store in the desired format.

A DW creates a centralised, controlled environment for reporting data. The downside is there is a high failure rate for warehouse activities, predominantly because they're driven by the IT department not the business, and often they don't have a specific goal in mind and so tend to meander aimlessly for some time, loading in data that is often not used. The other issue is there is no opportunity for reuse because the format of the data in the warehouse is typically formatted for reporting only – leaving little opportunity to integrate data with other systems. To be successful the warehouse must be built as part of a business project.

There are two principle design architectures for data warehouses thanks largely to the work done by William (Bill) Inmon and Ralph Kimball. Inmon is known as the "Father of Data Warehousing", while Kimball is known as the "Father of Business Intelligence".

Inmon believed in a "top-down" approach by establishing an enterprise wide data warehouse and then loading in as much data as possible believing that it might be used in the future. Kimball believed in a "bottom-up" approach by establishing smaller data marts to meet specific business outcomes and combining when necessary.

Structurally, Kimball utilised "star schema" with fact and dimension tables (effectively separating data from metadata and then using the star schema as a way of reconnecting the two). Inmon much preferred a relational schema where the data and metadata remain intact.

Both approaches have their strengths and weaknesses; there is no approach that is better than the other – it comes down to your organisation and which approach may be more successful.

Master data management

Master data management (MDM) is a different approach to data warehousing. The purpose of MDM is to create a shared data environment that is general purpose by nature.

Rather than extract and load data that may never be used, in MDM we're only interested in master data i.e. data that specifically relates to business objects and business transactions. Customers, Clients, Patients, Products, Sales – these are all examples of master data sets.

During the load process data analysis, data profiling and data cleaning are all performed to ensure the highest possible data quality. But rather than clean the data in the MDM database it is a better practice to clean the data in the source system. It is considered best practice (and common sense) not to allow bad data into the MDM database because this will become the source for historical reporting and future decision-making.

Data lakes

Data Lakes is an emerging alternative for large data management activities. When you warehouse data, it first must be analysed and cleaned to make sure that you only ever have fit for purpose data. This is a very timely and costly exercise but means in theory that the data is ready to be consumed.

With data lakes, the data is loaded into a centralised location with no cleansing. The data is stored as it comes. When the data is required for use it is analysed and cleansed on the fly.

The theory behind data lakes is often there is extensive work performed in cleaning data that is seldom or never used therefore it should be more cost effective to only clean when it is consumed.

Concerns have risen over data lakes in that it means people consuming the data must have a higher skillset in order to ensure the data is clean and ready for use. Other industry experts have given their support to data lakes as an opportunity to make use of technology to do the heavy lifting.

The challenge that I see with data lakes is often, when you're analysing data in order to determine its usefulness for a specific activity, you have to join data sets to see the full picture. But if some of the data you're looking at is dirty, then how do you gauge how useful it will be? Also, rarely in an organisation is there a single entry and exit for data. Typically there are multiple places where data can be extracted and with a data lake you would need to clean the data at every exit point leading to duplicate process management, which is hardly efficient.

I still believe that Master Data Management is a better approach as you're only managing data that is of interest, so the scope of activity is more reduced than a traditional data warehousing activity.

Data visualisation

The latest trend in data analytics is data visualisation. Your average user doesn't want to know the formula for binomial distribution - they just want the answer. So the best way of demonstrating the outcome of data analysis is with a graphical display. But vendors have gone a step further and made these graphical displays simple to use and powerful. If you're a spreadsheet guru then you know how to create graphs. Vendors have made these graphical displays dynamic and include statistical modeling functions. All you do is point the software at a data source and the tool largely does the rest. The simplicity is designed for any level of user (though ideally targeted at management) and may include a mobile device option for analytics on the go.

Chapter summary

By now you should have a good overall understanding of information management, knowledge management, data management, and how they interrelate. The single biggest challenge facing every organisation globally is data quality. Regardless of how many sophisticated computer systems are put in place, or back-of-house people paid to fix the data, the only way to truly make headway is through organisational culture change. Your Executive Management must understand the value of data as a corporate asset alongside other corporate assets such as buildings and furnishings, and understand the downstream costs in terms of technology, people and lost opportunities.

Organisations must adopt a "One Data" approach to data and information management in order to benefit from efficient and effective use of data to drive competitive outcomes.

For those of you who are visual learners below is a map illustrating the concepts covered thus far.

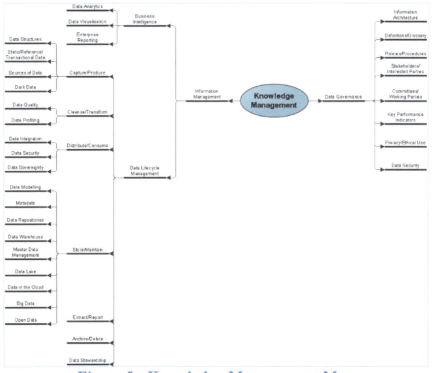

Figure 5 - Knowledge Management Map

As a final note, DAMA International have a large repository of resources relating to data management, including standards, educational material, and various publications. The IAIDQ likewise have a wealth of material on their website including formal accreditation. Information for both Organisations is in the references chapter of this book.

PART II: ONE DATA

"Data is the new oil!"

-Clive Humby, ANA Senior marketer's
summit, 2006

"Data is the new oil? No: Data is the new
soil!"

-David McCandless, TEDGlobal, 2010

CHAPTER 3: THE ONE DATA PATTERN

This chapter defines and describes the One Data pattern in detail. While there is no industry standard for the structure of a pattern, I've chosen to follow the structure established by Linda Rising (pattern expert amongst other things and co-author of *Fearless Change - Patterns for Introducing New Ideas*). Thus the structure is as follows:

The One Data Pattern	
Name	Name of the pattern.
Problem	Type of problem the pattern addresses.
Rationale	Reason why this pattern may be able to assist.
Assumptions	In order for the successful use of the pattern, what are the elements presumed to be in place.
Structure	Body of the pattern itself and details what needs to occur.
Resulting Context	Describes the expected outcome of the application of the pattern.

Table 6 – Pattern template definition.

Patterns aren't an exact science but they are a great way to encapsulate any repeatable process into something that can be followed almost like a work instruction or standard operating procedure.

Name
One Data – A pattern for data centric projects.

Problem
One Data can be used whenever you have any kind of data management activity. The components described in this pattern should be customised to suit the culture of your organisation, and the skills of the people who will be assisting you.

Rationale
It only takes a quick search of the Internet to see that a large proportion of projects fail (I've seen reports as high as two-thirds fail).

There are a number of factors that can cause a project to fail including:

	Common Reasons for Project Failure
i.	The project is led by IT and not the business
ii.	Lack of strategy
iii.	Failure to identify the problem
iv.	Poor data quality
v.	Poorly managed project
vi.	Failure to deliver the benefits identified
vii.	Failure to meet the stakeholder needs

Table 7 – Common reasons for project failure

This pattern will help you identify and manage all of these (and other) factors to deliver a successful outcome.

Assumptions

Tangible business outcome

You must have a tangible business outcome in order to use this pattern. Rationale: The majority of projects that are driven by IT fail. It is imperative that the business has a tangible problem that needs to be addressed in order to gain their support for your approach.

Access to People

You must have direct access to the people you identify on your project. Rationale: If you have to deal with an intermediary manager or supervisor each time you need access to key people, they will create a dependency bottleneck in your project and may affect your ability to complete the project on time and budget.

Project vs. Business as Usual

Often, to save costs, an organisation will insist on project staff who have been seconded from their business unit are required to continue some or all of their business as usual activities as well as project activities. For your project to be successful, key people who are seconded to the project must be as insulated from business as usual activities as possible. Rationale: Role tension between project and normal business operations may affect your ability to complete the project on time and budget.

Structure

Figure 6 - One Data pattern structure

One Data Lifecycle	
i.	Identify the problem
ii.	Create the vision
iii.	Design the solution
iv.	Implementation – leading the change
v.	Continual improvement

Table 8 – One Data Lifecycle

These elements are discussed further in this book.

Resulting context

The application of this pattern will:

- Help you gain a detailed understanding of the true nature of the problem at hand and establish the baseline target vision. This will also include identifying the benefits of the vision, and key performance indicators.

- Define the boundaries by which the problem must be resolved. These boundaries will consist of functional and non-functional requirements, and data design artifacts.

- If the solution requires software to be developed, then there will be enough information for the developer to develop a first cut solution. The end goal isn't to attempt to fix the problem in one foul swoop, but rather to solve the problem through the cycle of continual improvement.

- Establish the mechanisms that will be used to implement the solution, remembering that it's not just about the technical aspects but how you engage with the people that will be impacted.

- Putting controls in place to measure and monitor your key performance indicators.
- Establishing processes to review and refine the plan so as to lead back into the cycle of continual improvement.

CHAPTER 4: IDENTIFY THE PROBLEM

A problem can come from two sources – something that someone else brings to your attention, or something that you discover yourself. Regardless, the approach is the same. You must understand the true nature of the problem, which it is affecting, how it is affecting and why.

The outcome of problem identification is to write a clear and concise problem statement that captures the present state and the desired outcome.

Engage your Stakeholders early

No matter how you go about it, understanding the problem means having lots of conversations, and the best people to begin those conversations with are your stakeholders. ISO9000 Principles for Data Quality Systems also states the importance of engaging key people early, and maintaining that engagement throughout the process.

In an ideal world each major system would have a Business Owner and a Technical Owner. The Business Owner will have overall responsibility for the overall strategic direction of the system. The

Technical Owner will have overall responsibility for the efficient management and use of the system.

RACI

Figure 7 - RACI definition

RACI is tool to help identify the key people (or groups of people) that you need to communicate with, and in what context. It identifies the following categories:

R – Who is the person responsible for doing the activity.

A – Who is the final decision maker and therefore the owner of the activity.
C – Who should be consulted before, and throughout the decision making process.

I – Who needs to be told about the decision.

Here's an example based on the One Data pattern and the kinds of business and technology roles you might have:

Activities	Functional Roles				
	Analyst	Stakeholder	Developer	Tester	Change Manager
Problem Definition	R	A/C	I	I	I
Vision Statement	R	A/C	I	I	I
Solution Design	R	A/C	R	R	I
Implementation	C	A/C	R	R	R
Review & Refine	R/A	A/C	C	C	C

Figure 8 - Example RACI matrix

The Five Why's

The Five Whys methodology for problem solving is a very simple approach attributed to the Toyota Company back in 1970.

The process simply involves repeatedly questioning – or asking why (with 5 times being the rule of thumb). The premise behind five-whys is using simple questioning to dig deeper into a problem in order to find the root cause.

The results of each question can be represented graphically.

For example:

Figure 9 - An example of the five-why's approach.

Root Cause Analysis

When I grew up there was a television show called MacGyver. Every episode was an adventure, with lead character MacGyver (played by American actor Richard Dean Anderson) would find himself in some awkward situation, and escape required just enough ingenuity, a trusty pocket knife, duct tape, chewing gum and anything else he could scavenge from his surrounds. If you look around your organisation you're bound to find people fixing the symptoms of a problem, as MacGyver did, without attempting to find and fix the source. The problem (if you'll pardon the pun) is that so long as you address the symptoms, the cause is likely to continue with the risk of getting worse.

Root Cause Analysis (RCA). RCA is based on the premise that to truly fix a problem you must understand the problem from where it stems (i.e. the root). An RCA can be reactive or proactive. If you wait until a known issue has grown into a full-blown problem then that is reactive – you're reacting to the problem. However if you identify that there is an issue early and begin an RCA before it becomes a more serious problem then that is proactive problem management.

In order to undertake an RCA you must first answer these questions:

	RCA Learning's
i.	What is the problem?
ii.	How does the problem impact?
iii.	When does the problem occur?
iv.	Where is the problem?
v.	Who does the problem impact?

Table 9 – RCA Learning's

The following principles apply when undertaking an RCA:

	RCA Principles
i.	It's not a witch-hunt – there's no blaming anybody
ii.	Don't look for a quick fix – dig deeper!
iii.	Data is everything – identify the timeline of events leading up to the problem
iv.	Be specific – when someone complains "it's running slow" quantify "how slow is slow". Gather dates, times, and actions.
v.	Look for patterns. Are there other ways the problem can be caused? Does the problem impact multiple people or multiple environments?

Table 10 – RCA principles

Grounding assumptions

An all too common problem when working with a variety of people is establishing common ground. Often, during this process of understanding the problem it is easy to make assumptions about what we don't know or understand. It is important to identify assumptions and attempt, through the process, to ground them as either true or false and incorporate those learning's into the solution design.

To make assumptions visible create an assumption log where assumptions are not just recorded, but allocated to an individual to ground, and record what activity or learning's have come from analysing the assumption. The format for an assumption log looks something like this:

Assumptions Log
Assumption Reference Number
Category
Assumptions
Owner
Date
Assigned To
Date Resolved
Status
Actions

Table 11 – Elements of an assumptions log

Writing the problem statement

Now that we understand the problem, the final step is to write a problem statement. The problem statement is a concise explanation of the facts, issues, and risks and describes the desired future state. The problem statement does not suggest a solution.

Step 1: Capture the problem

i.   Write out as much about the problem as you know.
ii.   Use the questions in the section on Root Cause Analysis or the five-why's to expand your knowledge.
iii. Refine the problem based on information learned.

Step 2: Capture the desired future state

i.   What would it be like not having the problem?
ii.   Who needs to be involved in rectifying the problem?
iii. When does the problem need to be rectified?
iv.   Where does the problem need to be rectified?
v.   Refine the desired future state based on information learned.

Step 3: Putting it all together

i.   Start by aligning the refined problem state with the refined desired future state.
ii.   Create one problem statement for each problem.
iii. Your problem statement should only be a small paragraph (two or three sentences).
iv.   Resist the temptation to write a solution into your problem statement. Remember – your problem statement is designed to capture the essence of the problem in order to then determine the most appropriate course of action.

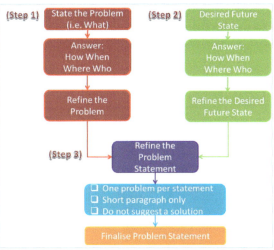

Figure 10 - Steps to writing a concise problem statement.

Review

Now that you have a better understanding of the problem you need to share your problem statement with the stakeholders and interested parties. This helps to not only confirm what you have learned throughout this process, but also helps to establish a trusting relationship.

Example problem statement:

There are lengthy delays in supplying Widgets to fulfill Customer Orders due to delays in the manufacturing and supply of parts by XYZ Parts Inc. The delay is impacting negatively on customer satisfaction resulting in loss of sales revenue and negative brand sentiment.

Chapter summary

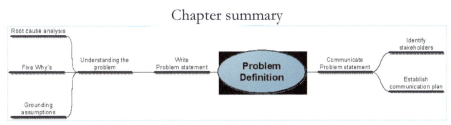

Figure 11 - Problem Definition Map

Understanding the root cause is imperative to designing an effective solution as this will help shape your requirements.

CHAPTER 5: CREATE THE VISION

Understanding the problem is the first part of finding a resolution. The second part is understanding the organisation strategy; its mission, values, and principles. These are important because they will help shape the design of the solution ensuring alignment with the organisation.

Writing the vision statement

Before embarking on solution design, consider the big picture – if your solution was complete, what would success look like? Like your problem statement, your vision statement should be concise and be optimistic – after all, it is your desired future state.

Review

Now that you have a vision statement you should share it with your stakeholders and interested parties to confirm that the solution matches their expectations.

You should also reaffirm that your vision is in line with organisational strategy and direction.

Example vision statement:

To fulfill all Customer purchases of Widgets and ship within 48 hours of payment.

Chapter summary

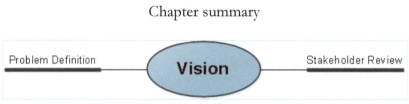

Figure 12 - Vision Statement Map

It doesn't matter how much time and money is put into a solution – if the users hate it then the organisation will never obtain the full benefit and the solution is likely to be considered a failure. Establishing a shared vision for the solution through collaboration with the stakeholders and key users will help generate further engagement. By branding the solution you effectively turn it into a product, which will help when "selling" it to Executive Management and the users.

CHAPTER 6: DESIGN THE SOLUTION

Requirements analysis

You know what the true problem is, and you have a vision for the future. But how do you get there? There isn't enough information yet to engage someone to build your solution, and if you were to buy a solution how would you determine which one will do the best job for the money you have to spend? I have witnessed plenty occasions where a product was purchased based on some high level concepts and slick sales presentations, only to see it fail or cost two or three times as much in customising it to fit the business. Rarely in these situations does the business actually obtain any tangible benefits.

The answer lies in requirements gathering. There are two forms of requirements – functional and non-functional.

Requirements offer the following benefits:

	Requirements Benefits
i.	Benefit definition and baselining
ii.	Project scoping

iii.	Budgeting
iv.	Scheduling
v.	Software design
vi.	Software testing
vii.	Documentation and training

Table 12 – Requirements benefits

Requirements fall into one of two categories:
i. Functional, and
ii. Non-functional

Non-functional requirements

Non-functional requirements are those that describe the environment that the solution must operate in. They include subjects such as:

	Non-functional Requirements
i.	Usability
ii.	Reliability
iii.	Performance
iv.	Scalability
v.	Supportability
vi.	Sociability
vii.	Security and Privacy

Table 13 – Non-functional requirements

Usability

Usability requirements describe how the system should operate. Common usability requirements include:

	Usability Requirements
i.	Specific functions should complete within a finite amount of time (e.g. Search will complete in less than 5 seconds).
ii.	All screens should have a common look and feel.
iii.	Screens should not allow data to be saved until all required fields have been completed.
iv.	All fields must be validated upon entry so as to ensure data completeness and accuracy.

Reliability

Reliability requirements describe the required level of resilience for planned and unplanned outages. Common reliability requirements include:

	Reliability Requirements
i.	The solution must not maintain any unsaved data in memory in case of power loss.
ii.	The solution must be available between certain hours (e.g. 0800 to 2000 Monday to Friday).
iii.	The solution must meet a minimum level of uptime. One such model is known as the "five-nines" model for high availability. Five-nines is an expression of the amount of time the system must be operational divided by the amount of time the business is

prepared to tolerate expected downtime expressed as a percentage. For example, let's suppose the business are expecting the system to be operational 16 hours per day, and prepared to tolerate 1 hour of downtime within the 16 hours. The calculation is Ao = (16 − 15) / 16 = 93.75% operational or "one-nine" on the five-nines scale.

Performance

Performance relates to the overall operation of the solution. Commonly included performance requirements include:

	Performance Requirements
i.	The solution must start within 10 seconds of being launched.
ii.	When performing a process, the solution must display a timer so as to indicate that a process is in fact running.
iii.	When producing a report, the report must complete within 5 minutes.

Scalability

Scalability is another mechanism of high availability and performance however it relates to the environment more so than the solution itself. Common scalability requirements include:

	i.	The solution must be scalable and extensible for acquisition or expansion of services through the provision of additional computing power.

Supportability

Supportability requirements define how the solution is to be managed, configuration changes and upgrades applied, and future enhancements released. Common supportability requirements include:

		Supportability Requirements
	i.	Any changes by the solution vendor must adhere to organisational change procedures (assuming you have them!).
	ii.	The solution vendor must provide 24x7x365 support.

Sociability

Sociability requirements are often forgotten about and simple compatibility between external components can break even the best-planned solution. Sociability requirements will be very specific to your organisation and the major hardware and software platforms in use. Be sure to consider, for Internet based solutions, what web browser version and supported plugins are required and whether or not they are compatible with those your organisation uses.

Common sociability requirements include:

		Sociability Requirements
	i.	The solution must be capable of operating on virtual infrastructure (you will need advice from your IT department to determine if this is a requirement).

ii.	The solution must be compatible with applications that form the Standard Operating Environment (SOE) including office productivity suite, email, Internet web browsers and other enterprise applications.

Security and privacy

Security and privacy requirements are incredibly important, as these will protect your solution from malicious intent and likewise protect your customers against unlawful use of their personal information.

Security requirements often relate to hardware and network connections; particularly where those connections link with the Internet. These requirements are usually the domain of your IT department. When it comes to evaluating products and services it's important to understand what capabilities are provided.

Privacy requirements include:

	Privacy Requirements
i.	The solution must provide an audit log of access for read and write operations including the identification of the user, the machine name, date and time, the operation executed and the result.
ii.	No information will be shared via email or social media.

Recently I received an anonymous text message giving me the pin code for a locked box at some obscurely named place. My then 15 year old Son jumped onto Google, and within seconds had identified that the message was from a coastal hotel about 90 minutes' drive away. We then deduced that the instructions were meant for someone else who was staying and would need to collect their key from the locked box. Armed with that information we could potentially have gained access to the hotel room. If there were two keys on the key ring then we could have stolen one to gain entry later. Clearly there is a data quality issue here in that either the mobile phone number was recorded incorrectly in their database or it was mis-entered in sending the message. Email and instant messaging (SMS text messages or web messenger tools) are not reliable, safe and guaranteed mechanisms for delivering important information.

Functional requirements

Functional requirements are those that describe the features of the solution in terms of its operation and intended behavior. This behavior may be expressed as services, tasks or functions the system is required to perform.

Data design

Understanding the data you have to work with is a vital component of any system design – after all – it's all about the data!
Data modeling is the process of understanding data – of taking data and providing context through meaning.

There are a number approaches to data modeling however there are two that I believe represent the best value in terms of creation and ongoing maintenance and being easy to comprehend by the business - Data flow diagrams, and relational data models.

Data Flow Diagrams

Data flow diagrams (DFDs) abstract away any system boundaries in order to show the flow of data within a business process or system. DFDs are an industry standard way of graphically mapping the core flows of information through business processes, and what business functions produce or consume data.

The main components of a data flow diagram are:

	DFD Shapes
Start	The Start shape is used to identify where in the flow to begin. Sometimes there are multiple start points, depending on what the triggering event or activity is.
Stop	The Stop shape is used to signify that the flow has ended successfully (i.e. without error).
Error	This is an alternative stop state, which can be used to indicate that the process cannot be completed because of some exception. For example, when we validate a Customer Order we might discover that this Customer has a bad track record of paying on time, and so they should not be permitted to make a purchase.
1.0 Process or Function	An activity, which is uniquely identified, defines some function or process. For example, you might have a function called 1.0 Fulfill Customer Order.
Data Process	Any activity that is processing, manipulating, transforming or otherwise producing data.

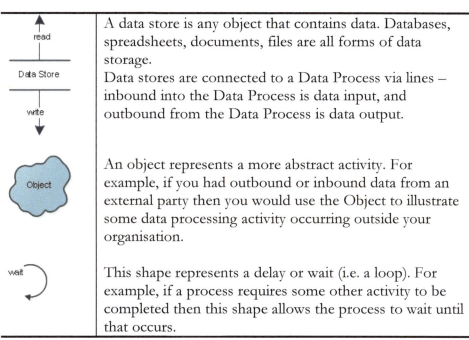 read / Data Store / write	A data store is any object that contains data. Databases, spreadsheets, documents, files are all forms of data storage. Data stores are connected to a Data Process via lines – inbound into the Data Process is data input, and outbound from the Data Process is data output.
Object	An object represents a more abstract activity. For example, if you had outbound or inbound data from an external party then you would use the Object to illustrate some data processing activity occurring outside your organisation.
wait	This shape represents a delay or wait (i.e. a loop). For example, if a process requires some other activity to be completed then this shape allows the process to wait until that occurs.

Table 14 - Common shapes for Data Flow Diagrams.

Here's a completed example:

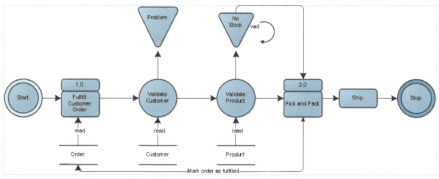

Figure 13- Example Data Flow Diagram.

Begin by sketching what you know on paper, and then share your diagram with your stakeholders and interested parties. Very quickly you will see your diagram flourish into a fairly composite overview of what information flows where.

Typically you would start with a high-level diagram (known as a DFD-0), then draw a more detailed diagram for each process. There's no limit to how "deep" you model, but most of the time 1-2 levels is sufficient. I usually only map the more complicated processes.

Relational Data Modeling

The data flow diagram is great for illustrating the movement of information but doesn't detail the interconnections between data elements. That's where relational modeling becomes very useful.

By its nature, relational modeling (or entity-relationship diagram – ERD) explores the main data elements (known as entities) and how they interconnect with other entities. ERDs are another industry standard method for graphically representing core data and the relationships between data sets.

There are five steps to creating a relational model:

	Relational Modeling Steps
i.	Identify the main entities
ii.	Identify the relationships
iii.	Define the key attributes
iv.	Create the model
v.	Refine the model

Table 15 – Relational modeling steps

Identify the main entities

Identifying the main entities involves examining real world objects. A Person, Product, and Location – these are all very common entities that can be derived simply by looking at the business processes and the information that is being shared (either on paper or electronically).

Identify the relationships

Identifying relationships involves understanding the interrelations between not only the entities, but the way in which the entities are used (otherwise known as cardinality).

You might have a customer order form that contains some of the customer information and allows the customer to stipulate all of the products they wish to purchase. This relationship is said to be "1 to many" between the customer and the products.

You might also have a list of products and a list of orders that each product has been ordered on. This relationship is said to be "many to many" as many products can belong to many orders.

Typically, each customer order would have one and only one tax invoice and a tax invoice can belong to one and only one customer. This relationship is said to be "one to one".

Define the key attributes

Once you know your entities and relationships you can define your attributes. Attributes are the specific characteristics (or data elements) that define an entity. If your entity is a customer purchase order form, then the attributes are the content of that form (e.g. customer name, address, contact information etc.)

As part of understanding the attributes is identifying what the unique identifier is. Typically each entity will have one primary attribute (or Primary Key). So for a customer you would have a "Customer ID" and this can be as simple as a counter of 1 to n where n is the total number of customers. The Primary Key is always identified with an underline.

When evaluating attributes you must consider what is mandatory and what is optional. Mandatory attributes are those that must be present – such as a Customer Name. Optional attributes are nice to have but not necessary.

It is also very handy to attempt to identify the type of data being captured in the attribute. If it's a date, call it a date. If it's numeric, state that it is numeric. If you attribute has a maximum size (which is rare if you're working with paper forms) then stipulate the size as well.

Understanding the attributes is very important when it comes to database and screen design and development later on, because the developers will need to know which fields will need to have data validation checks in place.

Create the model

A relational data model can either be expressed using business terms or graphically.
Below are the common shapes and their description:

E-R Diagram Shapes	
Entity1 PK **primary key** attribute1 attribute2	An entity represents a real world object that contains data. A form, a spreadsheet, a document are all examples of one or more entities. Entities contain attributes. An attribute is a specific data item. So if you had an Entity called Customer then you might have attributes such as First Name, Last Name etc.

⊣⊢	This shape represents 1 and only 1 entity may exist. If there is 0 or more than 1 then this is regarded as an error.
⊶⊣	This shape represents 0 or 1 entities may exist. If there are more than 1 entity then this is regarded as an error.
⊣<	This shape represents a minimum of 1 or more entities. If there is 0 then this is regarded as an error.
⊶<	This shape represents 0 or more entities.
PK	The Primary Key (or PK) represents a guaranteed unique identifier for any given entity. Using a primary key guarantees referential integrity by not permitting duplicate records. If you consider the Customer entity, how many people in the world have the name "John Smith?" When shipping the Order, how can you guarantee that the right person receives the right product? That's the value of the use of primary keys.
FK	The Foreign Key (or FK) represents the unique identifier of a related entity and is the glue that links one or more entities.

Table 16 - Common shapes for ER diagrams.

As an example, here's a very simplistic relational model for a Customer Order:

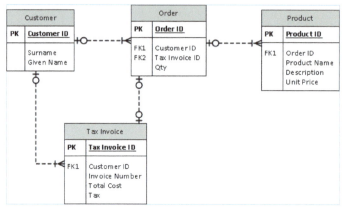

Figure 14 - Entity-Relationship diagram for a Customer Order.

From this example, narratively we can see:
- A Customer has a Surname and Given Name.
- A Customer may have 1 or more Orders.
- A Customer may have 1 or more Tax Invoices.
- An Order may only belong to 1 Customer (this is important as you don't want your Customers being billed for or receiving other people's Products!)
- An Order has a Qty.
- An Order may have 1 or more Products.
- An Order has 1 and only 1 Tax Invoice.
- A Product may only belong to 1 Order.
- A Product has a Product Name, Description and Unit Price.
- A Tax Invoice may only belong to 1 Customer.
- A Tax Invoice has 1 and only 1 Order.
- A Tax Invoice has an Invoice Number, a Total Cost, and a Tax.

From this model, we can also determine:
- How many of a particular Product is required (i.e. to manage stock levels)
- How much revenue is being generated and through which Products.

We can also produce a printed Tax Invoice complete with itemised product list. By multiplying the Qty by the Unit Price we can calculate (or derive) the total payable and any taxes.

Another way to represent the same information is in table form:

Object: Customer

Attribute	Description	Data Type	Size	Format	Mandatory?	Valid Values
Customer ID	Uniquely identifies a Customer	Numeric		PK	Y	Positive integers only
Surname	Customer's last name	Text			Y	
First Name	Customer's first name	Text			Y	
Customer Since	The date the person became a Customer	Date		Day-Month-Year	N	

Figure 15 - A tabular representation of an entity.

Refine the model

It's not uncommon to go through this process (particularly if you're primary source of information is paper form based) and wind up with an amount of duplication. Your Customer form will have customer details on it, your Purchase Order form would have some customer information on it, and your Delivery form will have customer details on it. The refinement process (also known as normalisation) is to merge related entities and attributes into one entity and references the entity by its Primary Key. So instead of having all those customer details on different forms have a single Customer entity with all of the customer details you need as attributes. Then whenever you need to refer to a specific Customer, you store their Customer ID (just like we did in the figure above). There are several levels of normalisation however the more your database is normalised the more complex it becomes to work with. Database developers can assist in further refining the database design during development.

Business process design

Business process design involves understanding the current state and designing the future state. There are a number of methodologies available and I have selected two commonly used approaches, which are Use Case Design and Business Process Management.

Use case design

Use cases are used in conjunction with user stories and involve describing the interactions between actors for a given function.

The main difference between a user story and a use case is a use case is predominantly describing a function or operation whereas a user story is describing what functions or operations a particular user will perform.

Whilst there is no standard as such for describing use cases, the following pattern may be useful.

Use case pattern

Use Case Pattern
This should be the entity name followed by an action verb. Example: Customer-PlaceOrder The name should adequately describe the process and should make sense to the business.
Description This is the goal or outcome to be achieved. It should include major business rules, and sources of information.
Actors List of actors involved in use case (as covered previously in this chapter).

Example: Customer	

Assumptions

A list of assumptions relating to this use case and any of its interactions. These are typically different to the assumptions identified during the problem statement definition phase, as these tend to be more detailed and more specific to the use case. Having said that, they should be captured on the assumptions log to ensure they are resolved.

Example:
1. It is assumed that the input file will never be empty.

User stories

These are the interactions that must occur between actors in order to achieve the goal. These are written in business language.

Example:
1. When the User clicks the Shopping Cart Icon,
   Execute ShoppingCart-Display.
2. When the User clicks the Home button,
   Execute Home-Display.

Exceptions

Any identified exceptions to the steps that may require additional management.

Example:
1. If the payment for the order is declined more than 2 times,
   Create and send an email to the support team including details of the exception.

Non-Functional

There may be non-functional requirements that are specific to this use case. Typically these would be to do with scheduling, and any volatility.

Example:
1. This use case needs to be highly secured as it will interact with payment gateways.

Table 17 - Use Case Pattern.

Actors

The first step in solution design is to understand who the target (or end state) actors are. Actors are roles within business function and are part of the Unified Modeling Language (UML) toolset. The information will be needed not just for solution design but also communication during and after the project has completed.

To identify actors start with the stakeholders. Next, find out the business functions involved and identify the people who perform those functions.

For example:
Customer
Supplier
Manufacturer

User stories

User stories are designed to capture a specific goal or outcome using business language. User stories take on the following format:

"As a <actor role>, I want <desire>, so that <outcome>."

For example:

Customer:
As a Customer, I want to be able to add a Product to my Shopping Cart, so that I am able to perform an online purchase.

As a Customer, I want to be able to pay for my order online using a variety of payment methods including credit card and PayPal.

Business Process Management

Business process management (BPM) is another approach to improving business processes and making them more efficient. BPM uses a lifecycle approach to understating the current state, identifying the desired future state, and then determining the steps required to get there.

Figure 16- Business process management lifecycle

Design

The design phase captures the current state business processes. Often the focus is on the process (i.e. what people do) not on the information flows. But using a data centric approach, you begin with your catalogue of information flows into the business unit and the outputs from the business unit. Included in the catalogue is where they come from and where they go to next.

Then begin to understand how the information is processed and document the functions are performed. You should also include how long each function takes to perform.

Once this catalogue is complete you can then design the desired future state. There may be multiple possibilities at this stage. Often, the current state and desired future state processes are captured in a diagram, and one common approach is Business Process Model and Notation (BPMN), which is covered next.

Model

Once you have your desired future state you need to "exercise" the design using real scenarios in order to test that what you have designed will work in practice. Through this process you will continue to refine your designs.

Execute

The execution phase is where you take your designs and convert them into runnable programs. You may either develop software that mimics the design or use a process automation engine.

Monitor

Once you begin executing your processes you need to monitor them to ensure that the desired outcomes are being achieved. This may be through the use of application audit logs, monitoring and management screens, reports, or checking the output data. If you use a process execution engine then it will provide much of this capability for you.

Optimise

I've made this all sound relatively simple – but the devil is in the detail and you don't won't really know how it will all work until you execute your processes and monitor. Over time you will need to make adjustments to improve performance and reliability; particularly as the volume of information being processed increases. Ultimately you may need to go back to the beginning and go through the steps again.

Business process model and notation

Business process model and notation (BPMN) is a modeling technique suited to capturing the desired future state in such a way that it can be executed via a process automation engine. BPMN models fit into the BPM Execution phase.

BPMN graphically represents business functions in the form of process flows.

Below is what I would consider to be the more commonly used symbols; the BPMN standard has additional symbols per category so it is worth the time to explore the standard in more detail.

Start Events	*Start events represent the beginning of a flow. There are many ways a flow could commence, some of which have been identified below.*
◯	Non-specific (i.e. generic) start event. Use this symbol to identify the start of a flow.
✉	Message triggered start event. For example, a process begins whenever a specific message is received – could be an email, or it could be an inbound telephone call from a customer.
🕐	Timer triggered start event. For example, a flow must begin at a specific time of the day.

| 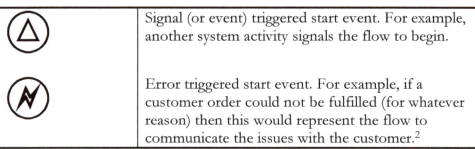 | Signal (or event) triggered start event. For example, another system activity signals the flow to begin. |
| | Error triggered start event. For example, if a customer order could not be fulfilled (for whatever reason) then this would represent the flow to communicate the issues with the customer.[2] |

Table 18 - BPMN Start events

End Events	**End events describe what activity occurs on conclusion of a flow.**
⬤	Non-specific (i.e. generic) end event. Use this symbol to represent the successful end to a flow.
⬤	End event with message trigger. This shape represents an end event that will send a message on termination.
⬤	End event with signal trigger. This shape represents an end event that will raise a signal in order to trigger the beginning of another flow.
⬤	This shape represents an end event that will raise an error on termination.

Table 19 - BPMN End events

Task Activities	**Task events represent some specific flow or activity.**
▤	Non-specific (i.e generic) business task. This represents a non-specific type of activity.
⚙	Service task. This symbol represents an automated or computerised activity. For example using a machine to fold mail and stuff into envelopes.

✉	Send task. This shape represents sending a message, possibly to trigger another process. For example, informing a customer that their order is ready to be collected.
✉	Receive task. This shape represents receiving a message and processing it. For example, the warehouse receiving a purchase order from a customer.
☞	Manual task. This shape captures an activity manually performed by a person. For example, picking stock off a shelf to fulfill a customer order.
☺	User task. This shape represents some activity performed by a user within a software application. For example, managing billing information in an accounting system.

Table 20 - BPMN Task activities

Gateway	*Gateways represent decision points in which there are multiple possible flows depending on the conditions.* *Gateways can also be used to merge multiple flows back into a single flow.*
◇X◇	Exclusive gateway. This shape represents an exclusive gateway where there are multiple flows but 1 and only 1 flow can be triggered. For example, while processing a customer order, if a call to a banking service to debit the customer account can either be successful and the order can be fulfilled, or unsuccessful and the order is not fulfilled.

---

[2] The BPMN symbols used are provided with permission from Trisotech Inc.

◇○◇	Inclusive gateway. This shape is used where multiple flows can occur in series. For example, once payment has been confirmed, the products purchased can be picked, then packaged, and finally shipped.
◇✚◇	Parallel gateway. This shape is used where multiple flows can occur simultaneously. For example, when payment is confirmed from the bank, the customer can be notified that the transaction was successful and the process to fulfill the order can begin at the same time.

Table 21 - BPMN Gateways

Flows	***Flows are used to connect shapes. There are a number of types of flows as summarized below.***
——————→	Sequence flow. This shape represents the transition from one step to the next.
o—————▷	Message flow. This shape represents the flow of information from one shape to another. You can indicate (via a name) what the type of information is being shared. For example, as part of a customer order purchasing process, there would be a flow of customer demographic data.
·········▷	Data flow. This shape represents data flowing from a task to a data object.

Table 22 - BPMN Flows

Data Objects	***A data object is something that contains data and information. Data objects can be represented many ways as summarised below.***
▯	Non-specific (i.e. generic) data object. This could be a spreadsheet or paper form. This could also represent a printed report.

	Data store. For example, this could be a database or a filing cabinet.
	Data collection. For example collecting information from a customer.

Table 23 - BPMN Data objects

Swimlanes	*Swimlanes identify the core business function or role that relates to a process. Flows are used to show any interactions between functions or roles.*
Pool	Pools are a container for one or more swimlanes and logically group related processes flows into one core function.
Lane	Swimlanes encapsulate a single process flow that represents a specific role e.g. a customer.

Table 24 - BPMN Swimlanes

Subprocess	*Subprocesses help simplify the design of complicated process flows.*
	Collapsible subprocess. Graphically the process can be expanded or collapsed so as to hide away the process components making the overall diagram easier to view.
	Transaction. This shape represents a transaction. For example, you might wrap a flow that calls the bank to debit a customer bank account inside a

Table 25 - BPMN Subprocess

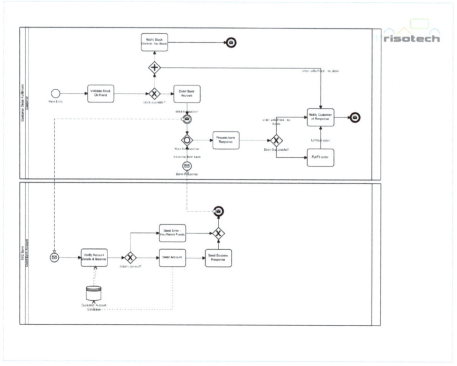

Figure 17 – Customer Order Fullfillment

Let's walk through the example above. Everything begins with the Customer and the Main Entry start flow. From there, the stock quantity is validated to ensure there is sufficient to fill the Order. If there is insufficient stock then a message is sent to the Stock Control team so they know to order more. A message is also sent to the Customer informing them that the purchase can't be made due to insufficient stock.

If there is sufficient stock, a message is sent to the Customer's nominated bank to debit their account. If the account doesn't have sufficient funds then an error message is returned. Otherwise the account is debited the amount and a success message is returned.

If the account was not successfully debited then a message is sent to the Customer to let them know they didn't have sufficient funds to clear the purchase.

Otherwise, the Order can be fulfilled and the Customer is notified of a successful transaction.

As you can see from this example, process flow mapping is a very simple yet powerful tool and can be used to map both the current and future state business process flows.

There are a number of commercial platforms that can take a BPMN diagram like the above and convert into a functioning computerised process without requiring any software development.

Gap analysis

The final part of any good design is to step back and look for holes – otherwise known as undertaking a gap analysis. Undertaking a gap analysis is a simple process of comparing what you know about the current state (i.e. the problem), what future state elements have been identified through the design process, and then confirming that the two align. The gap analysis can be managed with a simple spreadsheet with the following columns:

Gap Analysis Log
Present State
Transition Steps
Future State
Issues
Resolution
Date Resolved
Resolved By

Table 26 – Gap Analysis log elements

It is worth undertaking the gap analysis in a workshop format including all of the relevant people. I usually run these workshops similar to a retrospective (discussed later in the book).

Present state

In the spreadsheet, list all of the present state issues as identified in the problem statement work.

Future state

In the spreadsheet, list all of the future state requirements as identified in the vision statement incorporating the organisation strategy and architecture principles where relevant.

Transition state

In the spreadsheet, identify the design components and decisions that have been made to transition the present state issues to the future state vision. This includes any of the design elements from the One Data pattern. Is there anything missing? Ask yourself – what could make the solution fail, and what needs to be done to prevent these potential failures from occurring.

Issues

Record issues identified in this column in the spreadsheet. Use business terms and phrases and keep the content succinct.

Resolution

This column in the spreadsheet is for recording what the resolution for the issue will be.

Resolved by

It is important that every issue is assigned to a responsible person to lead the design of the resolution. Record the name of the responsible person in this column.

Resolution date

It is handy to document the date when a design resolution has been completed.

Architecture principles & sourcing models

When looking to procure technology there are a few things that need to be considered. First and foremost - what are the architecture principles of your organisation? Not surprisingly - many Organisations do not have well defined architecture principles and so often we see mash up technology with differing solutions that are complex to support.

If nothing else, consider reuse vs. build vs. buy and what order to apply them in.

Reuse vs. Build vs. Buy

Reuse

Reusing existing technology is usually the least expensive option. The knowledge and skills required should already exist. Where it can get costly though is when you try and make a solution do something that it wasn't intended for, or trying to expand the solution beyond its capabilities. Support can become very costly and there is a risk that you void whatever warranty you have with the vendor (if it's a procured solution).

Often though, Organisations purchase technology and then underutilise it. Desktop and Server virtualisation are examples of technology solutions that attempt to resolve the underutilisation of computer hardware, and when managed effectively, can significantly reduce the total cost of ownership relating to these devices.

Depending on the requirements for the new solution, there may already be a solution being used so it's very important that Organisations have a documented list of technology products in use, including the cost, licensing requirements, and when the solution will become end of life (typically 3-5 year for hardware, 5-7 years for software).

Build

This is more for software than hardware. Assuming your organisation has software development expertise then this is always an option worth considering. You will need to consider the size of the solution required vs. the time frame for delivery vs. the workload and priorities of your development team.

The cost of building a software solution may be significantly cheaper than buying however if the time to build a completed system is six months, twelve months or eighteen months plus then your window of opportunity may significantly decrease and with that the benefits associated with the solution also decrease and you risk having a solution that is of no commercial benefit. In order to determine if this is the right option you need to know what your opportunity timeframe is (i.e. time to market). Once you have determined this, and you obtain an estimate for the delivery of your in-house solution plus the costs associated with ongoing support and maintenance, you can then determine if this is the best approach.

One of the often over looked benefits of an in-house solution is the knowledge of the organisation is not only used in the design and build but is further enriched by the people involved.

Another significant benefit is you can get away with a less defined set of requirements and "tweak as you go". This agile approach means the cost of variation is low.

Buy

Buying a solution (hardware or software) can be the most costly approach but the tradeoff is you have greater control over time to market.

You will need to have complete and accurate requirements in order to either find the closest fitting solution, or have one custom developed. As with any custom build, any variation can be costly both in terms of dollars but also time to market.

You will need to consider any licensing requirements and make sure these aren't exceeded.

Unless you are looking at a fully hosted solution (i.e. "in the cloud") then you will also need to consider hardware requirements for the solution and ensure these are met (if you got with a hosted solution then the hosting company owns and manages the hardware on your behalf for a fee).

In contrast with an in-house solution, the knowledge associated with the inner workings of the solution is retained by the vendor. If you require further enhancements then you will need to pay the vendor and this can be expensive.

Sourcing models

Architecture principles are one set of guides you can use. Another are the sourcing models of in-sourced vs. out-sourced vs. co-sourced and thee can apply to both hardware and software.

In-sourced

In-sourced and in-house are one and the same.

Out-sourced

When you choose to buy an external product or service this is known as out-sourcing.

Co-Sourced

When you in-source you retain the knowledge associated with the solution (otherwise known as intellectual property or IP). When you out-source you lose the IP to the vendor.

Co-sourcing is a model where you still engage with a vendor for your solution however you also involve your own organisational people in a collaborative environment where knowledge transfer can occur. Co-sourcing also helps contain the costs by utilising existing people and skills.

The risk with co-sourcing is the vendor not engaging, which can result in the implementation taking longer, and potentially increasing costs.

By involving your own people in the implementation you have people who are then in a position to support and maintain it moving forwards.

Third party contracts

When establishing contracts with third parties, there are a few things to consider in regards to billing and payment methods and penalty clauses.

Billing and payment options are usually either fixed price fixed time, or time and materials.

Fixed time, fixed price contracts

With a fixed time and price contract, the third party is making a promise to deliver a completed service before an agreed date and within an agreed set price. In order for the third party to be able to determine the date and price they will require detailed information about the service required. Once the timeframe and price have been agreed to they form the basis for the delivery of the contract. If you decide after that point that you want to make a change to the service such that the timeframe or cost could be impacted then the third party will consider this a variation to the contract and charge you accordingly. You should also ensure that there is a penalty clause in your agreement should the third party fail to deliver as promised. I have experienced projects where a software vendor failed to deliver but because there was no penalty clause in the contracts there was no way to seek compensation without involving the law.

Fixed time and price contracts are more traditionally used for projects because, by their very nature, they put pressure on delivering on time and to schedule and so you're more likely to get a result sooner.

Time and materials contracts

These contracts offer much greater flexibility than fixed time and price contracts. These are typically charged on a daily or monthly fixed rate for the people required to undertake the work. Delivery schedules exist however there is less impetus to meet them; it's up to you to minimise changes to project scope that could delay final delivery.

Time and materials contracts are often used when the requirements aren't very firm. Quite often, support arrangements are time and materials due to the nature of them only being called upon when required.

You can still include a penalty clause however the focus will be more on the quality of the outcomes provided as opposed to being completed on time.

Chapter summary

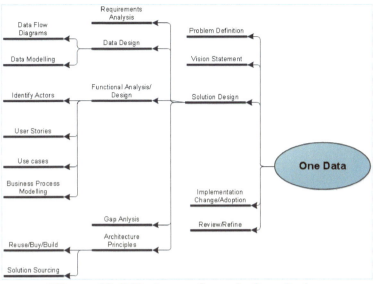

Figure 18- Mind map for solution design

By now you should have a very good idea of what is involved in designing a solution. Getting the design right is imperative for a successful outcome; don't underestimate the amount of time this can take to complete. Having access to the right people is also important. Sometimes there can be a temptation to reduce the amount of time required by adding more people. Again it depends on the size of the project, but adding more can impede your progress more than it assists and you risk overlap and duplication of effort. A common approach is to break the project design effort into streams of work, some of which can be run in parallel. So long as there is good communication between streams, this can be quite effective, and to minimise any duplication make sure there are clear demarcation of roles, responsibilities and deliverables.

CHAPTER 7: IMPLEMENTATION – LEADING THE CHANGE

Change and adoption is arguably the most important phase of any implementation of a new system. It is vitally important that the users of the new system are prepared to effectively use the system. Even the best made plans can be undone if the users refuse to use the system, or if the solution fails to meet their needs. Change and adoption begins early in the project beginning with understanding the problem and the vision, and continues right throughout the solution design phase with understanding the benefits and determining the value proposition for the new system, and then through into implementation.

You're now at the stage where you have your detailed requirements including your data needs and now need to look at options for implementing the design. This chapter discusses these options in more detail

Elements of success

There are a number of characteristics of successful projects; some of the important ones are discussed below.

Planning

"Failing to plan is planning to fail"

- Alan Lakein

My Father-in-law was taught in his Army years *"Proper Preparation and Planning Prevents Piss-Poor Performance"* otherwise known as the "7-P's of success" (please excuse the language). As someone who has worked on many projects – I get this. Regardless of what approach you intend to take, it is critical to the success of your project that you take the time to properly plan all of the activities that produce output and achieve outcomes.

Methodology

To help you with your planning, it's important to have a clear methodology for managing your project. There are a number of project methodologies available divided into waterfall and agile methodologies:

Waterfall methodologies

Focus on schedules, tasks and deadlines. Typically, core activities occur in sequence waiting for the prior one to be completed. Critics will tell you that waterfall methodologies are slow and cumbersome however if managed properly then projects can be delivered on time and budget with minimal scope creep. PRINCE2 and PMBOK are examples of this approach to project management.

Agile methodologies

Focus on the team self-directing. Work is scheduled based on priority and occurs in parallel in a cyclical fashion. There is latitude for the business to make changes as they go along. Critics of agile methodologies will tell you these projects never complete due to this cyclical nature, resulting in time and dollar blowouts. Scrum is an example of an agile methodology.

Many organisations are employing hybrid approaches by encapsulating agile development activities with waterfall like control mechanisms and these tend to be highly successful. Regardless of the approach it is vitally important that your project team all understand their roles and responsibilities and what is expected of them.

Project methodology proficiency requires training, certification and experience and there are a number of course providers available globally. Later in this book I discuss the Agile Manifesto which is the basis for all agile methodologies.

Testing

Testing is a crucial component of any successful solution delivery. There are various kinds of testing but the more typical ones are:

Unit testing
Undertaken by programmers to ensure that their programs are free from bugs (i.e. defects). How much time to spend unit testing depends on the complexity of the component being developed. I tend to use a percentage of the estimated development effort as a guide so for low complexity item I recommend 20%, for a medium complexity item I recommend 40% and for a high complexity item I recommend 60%. Factors that influence these figures include the level of skill and experience the developers have, and how well defined and documented the design is. So if a high complexity item is estimated to take 5 days to develop then an additional 3 days should be allocated for testing.

System testing
Often undertaken by a senior developer or senior analyst or test analyst to ensure that all of the interactions between components is functioning correctly. Often called "end-to-end" due to the nature of the testing. In terms of how long testing should take, I use 20% of the total

estimated development effort as a guide. So if the total development effort is 90 days then 18 days should be allocated to system testing.

Acceptance testing

Also known as User Acceptance Testing (or UAT), this testing involves your business users and the primary goal is to ensure that all of the business outcomes have been met. UAT is incredibly important because once you sign off on UAT you are stating that the system has been delivered and is fit for purpose. If your solution is being developed in-house then it's not such a big deal. But if you're working with a vendor then there are usually contractual obligations that come with UAT sign off. If you rush UAT in order to meet a deadline (which happens all too frequently) and you discover during or after implementation that there are issues then it may be costly to have them corrected. For these reasons, I recommend 40% of the design and development time be allocated for UAT. So if the design was 20 days and development was 90 days the UAT should be 44 days.

Proper testing is time consuming and therefore costly and is the first place that Organisations look to cut down when a project is behind schedule. Ironically testing is the one activity that can prevent costly failures during and after implementation.

The ISO 29119 Standard for Software Testing defines the components of test planning, how to test, and how to document testing and test results.

Documentation

Documentation is a valuable output from any project and you may have noticed that each step in the One Data process has generated documentation. But don't think of documentation as being static. Rather, think of documentation as something that is organic and therefore able to change over time; documentation that isn't maintained becomes useless the more the system changes after implementation.

Communication

One thing you will notice throughout this book is the theme of communication. I can't stress enough how important it is to communicate effectively – poor communication is a key contributing factor to project failure. When you communicate, consider the person or group you are speaking to – how will they interpret what you are saying? Try and avoid speaking jargon to non-technical people, and only use jargon around technical people if you are confident that you understand what it means.

One vital aspect of communication is when you are working with vendors from another country. You need to be very clear about your use of the vocabulary of your workplace because the same words may have different meanings to foreign vendors. Without clarification you risk wasting valuable time and dollars on redesign or reconfiguration of your system. This is where having a corporate glossary comes in handy.

Reporting and monitoring

Successful projects maintain accurate documentation of time and dollars – how much is allocated at the beginning and how much is being spent. This enables forecasting of what skills will be required as the project progresses, and whether or not there will be sufficient funds to complete. Keeping a project on time and on budget is the responsibility of the Project Manager.

Maintaining documentation is pointless unless it is shared therefore it is important to keep your stakeholders informed of your progress; they're the ones you will have to go back to if you need decisions made, more time or more money so they need to be actively involved an informed.

It is also important to maintain transparency; particularly if things aren't going quite as you had expected. Make sure you inform your stakeholders if there are issues, and where possible provide one or more alternative solutions.

People

Having the right team of people involved in your project is critical to its success. When recruiting team members you should consider not just the skills required but the cultural fit. Leaders, directors, doers, collaborators are all characteristics of people that you will need. A more detailed breakdown of the kinds of roles that may be required can be found later in this book.

"The right people, with the right skills, at the right time"

Continual improvement

Implementing change is one thing but embedding change is another. To maintain success beyond implementation you need to instill a culture of continual improvement within the team. One approach to continual improvement is the Plan-Do-Check-Act (PDCA) methodology.

Plan-Do-Check-Act

Walter Andrew Shewhart (physicist, engineer and statistician) established a model for obtaining knowledge through learning's, and then applying that knowledge for continual improvement. PDCA (and Deming's Plan-Do-Study-Act adaptation) is simple yet effective, and fits neatly within the agile methodology.

Figure 19 - Shewhart's Plan-Do-Check-Act cycle.

There are four components to the PDCA cycle:

Plan

Begin by determining the desired outcome and prepare a plan of attack. You need to consider your approach, frameworks, tools, and people required, and establish a project plan including key milestones and dates. Importantly – determine what success looks like and how you will measure it in terms of key performance indicators.

Do

Execute the plan, and begin monitoring the results. Collate process data for later analysis.

Check

Compare the outcomes against the plan and use the results gathered during the Do step to gauge progress. Graphs and charts are ideal mechanisms for observing data measurements.

Act

Now is the opportunity to review the plan and undertake an agile retrospective as follows:

     i.   What worked well?
     ii.   What didn't work so well?
     iii.   What should be continued?
     iv.   What should be discontinued?
     v.   Are there any remaining knowledge gaps?

When running a retrospective it is important to invite as broad a cross section of people involved in the project as possible. It is also critical that key decision makers are present – you never want to walk out of the retrospective with recommendations that require additional authorisation as this slows down the agile process. Bring along as many project artifacts as possible, plus the results from the analysis performed in the Check stage. Plan to have these retrospectives frequently – weekly at a minimum for a fixed amount of time so as to remain focused.

Use the information collected during the retrospective to alter the plan in readiness for the next improvement cycle, and communicate any changes to systems and processes to everyone involved.

The aggregation of marginal gains

The new General Manager and Performance Director for Team Sky Cycling, Dave Brailsford, faced a daunting challenge in 2010 - to be the first British team to win the Tour de France.

Dave believed in the value of the "aggregation of marginal gains"; that if you make a series of small (i.e.1%) improvements in everything you do, the sum of these will be something much more substantial.

The notion of marginal gains fits neatly with the agile methodology and lean thinking. Instead of trying to find one or two significantly large improvements, focus on keeping the solution simple and look for quick wins; particularly during your project retrospective.

Team Sky not only won the Tour de France in 2012, but Team Sky also won more than 70% of the cycling medals in the 2012 Olympic Games, and then won the Tour de France again in 2013.

Chapter summary

This chapter explored the One Data pattern in detail. Hopefully by now, you have the knowledge necessary to begin on your next data management project. Below is a process flow diagram of the One Data pattern.

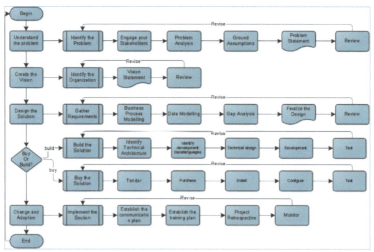

Figure 20 - Process flow diagram for the One Data pattern.

PART III: LEADERSHIP & COMMUNICATION

"If you don't know where you are going, you might wind up someplace else."

– Yogi Berra

CHAPTER 8: TEAM STRUCTURE AND SKILLS

We discussed in a previous chapter on the importance of people in making your project a success. This chapter looks at some of the key project roles and what value they bring to the project.

Project Sponsor

Description
The role of the project sponsor is to be the advocate for the project. The project sponsor will be an information conduit between the Executive Management team and the project team via the Project Manager. If there are issues raised by the project manager (such as going over budget or time) then these need to be addressed quickly in order to not hold up the project schedule. Ideally, the project sponsor will be an Executive Manager from the business.

Competence

Communication is key in this role, ensuring that the organisation knows exactly where the project is up to at any given time.

Typical outputs include

None.

Project Manager

Description

The role of the project manager is to ensure on time and on budget delivery of a solution. Managing schedules, tracking expenditure, recruiting staff are all typical functions of the project manager. Importantly, they also act as the primary communication channel between the project team and the organisation. Typically the project manager will submit regular status reports and present any risks, issues or concerns that could otherwise impact on delivery.

Competence

Planning, organising, coordinating and scheduling are all key competencies. Business acumen is important in terms of understanding the project importance to the organisation. Budgeting, time management, communication and leadership skills are paramount.

Typical outputs include:

This largely depends on what methodology is used, however typical outputs include business cases, project initiation, execution and closure documents, budgets, schedules, and actual performance against benchmarks (often using key performance indicators).

Solution Architect

Description

A solution architect works with the design of IT solutions based on requirements from the business, making use of existing IT capabilities and services in the organisation.

Solution architects have a special responsibility to reuse existing functions and services. They align new solutions to the current architectural principles regarding standards and integration in the organisation. They balance the functional and non-functional requirements with necessary prioritisations and compromises. The goal for the solution architect is the success of the current project, in addition to how well the project aligns to the architectural principles and how well it reuses existing capabilities.

When Organisations move from traditional applications to integrated solutions and services, the role of the solution architect becomes more and more important. The role of the solution architect is clearer in larger projects, particularly when many systems are involved. If the project is small or the application is isolated, this role may not be necessary in the particular project.

Competence

Broad and general technical knowledge, as well as deep competences in aspects such as technical infrastructure, database design, service orientation. Solution Architects should have experience (and preferably certification) in an enterprise architecture methodology such as TOGAF[3] or Zachman.

Typical outputs include

Application diagrams, system maps, service interfaces, technical interfaces, integration strategies.

Business Analyst

Description

Business Analysts (may be known as Business Architects) work very close to the business and understand in detail how the organisation works. They are active in modeling processes in the organisation and support solution architects with analysis and requirements on new or existing solutions. They understand how the IT systems support the business and suggest improvements together with enterprise architects.

---

[3] TOGAF® is a registered trademark of The Open Group.

Business Analysts are active in ongoing projects in the organisation using their influence to ensure that projects deliver benefits to the business in an optimal way.

Competence
Deep knowledge in the business; process modeling; requirement analysis; workshop facilitation skills.

Typical outputs include
Process maps, use cases, information models.

Developer

Description
If the solution is in-sourced then you will require development experience. The role of the developer is to take the requirements as defined by the Solution Architect and Business Analyst and translate them into functioning applications. There are a vast number of programming languages, tools and techniques available and your IT department can assist you in terms of understanding which is the best fit for the technology in use. How many developers depends on the size of the project, the delivery timeframe, and how much you are prepared to spend money wise.

Competence
Systems analysis and design experience is essential in whatever the chosen programming language has been selected. Most organisations require a developer to have completed a tertiary course in software engineering. Communications skills are important as is time management.

Typical outputs include
Technical solution design documentation, program source code, evidence of unit testing (test cases, results) and a functional application.

Test Coordinator

Description

Depending on the size and complexity of your project you may need a test coordinator. The role of the test coordinator is to coordinate all of the testing activities that are required, ensure that adequate testing is performed and issues are documented and resolved. The test coordinator will need to coordinate with the project team and the business users as part of acceptance testing. The test coordinator may be required to manage the testing environments with support from your IT department.

Competence
Planning, scheduling and communicating are critical competencies of this role. It is desirable to have a test coordinator who has sound business and technology knowledge, and is familiar with test processes and tools.

Typical outputs include
Test plans, test cases, testing schedules and supporting documentation.

Release Manager

Description
For large or complex Organisations you may benefit from having a change manager. This role helps coordinate the implementation of your solution into the business units. Depending on your project there may be a system outage required so the release manager would liaise with the business units impacted to ensure any outage occurs at a time of least impact, and that the business has appropriate controls in place during the outage. The release manager may also be the first point of call should there be any deployment issues wither during implementation or after the solution has been enabled. For this reason, the release manager needs to be actively involved in the project.

Competence
Planning, scheduling and communicating are critical competencies of this role. The release manager must have very good stakeholder negotiation and influencing skills. It is desirable that the release manager has a good overall knowledge of the business and technology in use.

Typical outputs include

Implementation schedules, resources required, contingency plans in case there are issues.

Data Analyst

Description
The role of the data analyst is to understand at a field level, the context, structure and use of data. The data analyst must understand where the data came from, and how it is consumed, and is a key contributor in new data management activities.

Competence
A data analyst must be proficient in database technologies, and structured query languages. Communication skills are very important as they must be able to translate what is occurring at the data level back to the business level. Technical knowledge and skills in a number of different database technologies so as to be able to map data between disparate systems.

Typical outputs include
Result data from writing queries, data model documentation and development, specifications for software development work, and expert knowledge in data.

Data Scientist

Description
The data scientist is an evolutionary step beyond the pure data analyst field. The data scientist uses advanced mathematical and statistical modeling techniques in order to derive additional value out of the data in a way that the business can understand. Data scientists are often researchers who have specific domain knowledge such as healthcare.

Competence
Very strong statistical and mathematical skills coupled with advanced structured query language skills are a must. Skills in statistical languages

such as R and scripting languages including Python are desirable. Familiarity with data visualisation tools is highly regarded.

Typical outputs include
All ofthose of a data anlyst, plus the design and development of one or more statistical models and the implementation of these models as part of a BI toolset for the business.

The Agile Manifesto

The Agile movement has been in existence since the 1950s when adaptive software development processes were first seen. Since then there have been a number of methodologies come into play with a common theme of *iterative design* and *rapid prototyping*, both of which are designed to provide the customer with a tangible outcome sooner (rather than later as occurs in traditional *waterfall* projects).

Though created for more efficient software development, the principles of the agile methodology can be applied to any activity.

So what is agility?
- Rapid and adaptive response to change
- Effective communication among all stakeholders
- Involving the business in the team
- Empowering the team so that it is in control of the work performed

The agile methodology revolves around twelve core principals as defined in the Agile Manifesto, ten of which are generic.

Continuous delivery of valuable outcomes

Keeping the customer engaged is essential for a successful outcome, and one of the best ways to achieve this is by early and continuous delivery of outcomes. Even if things aren't going as well as you'd like, if the customer has been involved along the journey, then they're more likely to be sympathetic, recognise the challenges you face and provide their own support in order to make progress. After all – they're the ones who want the outcome so it is in their best interests to be an active participant.

Changing requirements are welcome

From the moment I first became a programmer on a project, I was taught that scope creep is evil and should never be allowed. Is it fair and reasonable that we can document all of the requirements at the beginning of the project, and then never deviate? How would that work out for an 18 month project? The answer is – it doesn't. The pace of change means Organisations need to be agile which means projects need to be reasonably flexible so as to allow for change mid-stream. The best way to manage scope change is to document the requirements, determine the cost impact in terms of time and people and then present the change to your stakeholders for their consideration and approval. If the change means the project will take additional time to complete then the stakeholders will need to accept that outcome.

Bring front-of-house and back-of-house together

This might sound kind of obvious, but the best results come from bringing the project team and the business users together. There's nothing worse than spending 18 months on a project only to deliver an outcome that nobody wants to use. The ultimate determination of success or failure is the adoption of the business users (i.e. front-of-house). If you have buy-in from your business users in your solution, then they will become the sales persons for the solution to other staff enabling the culture shift required for successful adoption of your solution, and the timeframe for adoption will be significantly less than if you drop the solution on the business users with little or no prior engagement.

Trust in the project team individuals to do their job

Let's face it – people are hired for a reason. They possess skills or knowledge that you require in order to achieve your outcomes. To get the most from your people you need to trust them. Create a culture of openness and transparency, listen to their ideas and suggestions, and incorporate their recommendations.

Face-to-face communication

Email is great for communication with people, right? Wrong! Regular, face to face discussions are by far the best way to communicate within your project team and stakeholders. Email should only be used to summarise discussions and action items. Avoid hallway and telephone conversations, but if they occur always follow up with a summary email.

One of the best tools is a regular (i.e. weekly or daily) standup where everyone involved comes together to discuss the plans for the next period of activity, update on progress, and raise any issues or concerns. These are ideally no longer than 15minutes (the term stand-up literally refers to making everyone stand as a way of encouraging a short discussion) and it's important that everyone has an opportunity to speak.

Is it as simple as it can be?

This is actually my personal mantra. Is it as simple as it can be. At all times, if you are discussing a problem, a challenge, an issue, etc. and you find the discussion going around in circles then that's a great opportunity to stop – pause – and reflect.

Some handy questions to consider - Why does it seem so complicated, what are we doing wrong, is there a better way, is the requirement reasonable and achievable, how can we simplify?

The best designs come from self-organising teams

This goes hand-in-hand with trusting your team to do its job. A self-organising team is one in which there is equal power and ownership. Openness and transparency lead to a sense of freedom to contribute ideas and suggestions and from these come innovation.

Self-organised teams manage their own workload. They all know and have access to the task schedule and take it upon themselves to take on required tasks, update on progress, escalate any issues, and sign-off on completed work. If a task requires rework then they take that on as well. They require mentoring not managing.

Take the time to be retrospective

At the end of each logical phase, stop and reflect -What worked, what didn't work, what we should never do, what should we always do?

When holding a retrospective there are a few rules to help it run smoothly:

	Retrospective Principles
i.	**Set the scene**

	- "No sacred cows", "no elephants in the room." The discussion must be free from antagonism. Everyone has an opinion, a point of view and must feel safe to be able to speak their truth without fear of retribution. This can be quite daunting for some (particularly the introverted personality types). - Insist on only one person speaking at a time, and ask participants to raise their hand if they wish to contribute. - Encourage discussion but keep it short. Ideally no more than 5mins per discussion item. - Create a "Parking Lot" to record discussion elements that require further investigation, or if the current topic appears to be going around in circles.
ii.	**Review the facts** - You can't manage what you can't measure so bring along whatever metrics, measures, issues register, assumptions register, decisions and actions register, sample input and sample output.
iii.	**Generate insight** - Question everything in order to completely understand the good and the bad. This will expose any knowledge gaps that can then be added to the parking lot for follow-up.
iv.	**Identify Actions** - Decide what actions are required, and assign them to a participant. Keep a register of decisions and actions and review at the next retrospective.

Table 27 – Retrospective principles

Appreciation is the key to success

Here's a visual (with thanks to the British comedic group Monty Python) - a man, appearing to have found his way home after being marooned on an island; his clothes ripped and torn, his hair long and his beard over grown, strains to maintain balance as he wades and then staggers through wave after wave before finally making it to the beach. As he approaches, he collapses on the sand - breathless from his efforts. He looks up and begins to speak.

   "It's...." - and then he is cutoff as the credits roll (okay so if you didn't get the visual you can watch the clip here "http://www.youtube.com/watch?v=zJpJbL6Pzjo").

   Have you ever felt like you've just run a marathon because someone has asked you for something (and it's always urgent!) You hand over the completed request only to be responded with a casual "thanks". Feel appreciated? Of course not - and why would you.

   True appreciation comes from not just use of basic manners (i.e. use of "please" and "thank you"), but from demonstrating to the individual that their effort (however arduous) is truly appreciated; that there is value and meaning.

   Dr Jason Fox in his book "the Game Changer" identifies that people intrinsically want to know that their contribution is meaningful, and that they feel as though they are making a positive difference to their organisation. Often the organisational approach to motivation is through formalised reward and recognition programs (such as employee of the month) and cash bonus payments. Whilst these can work, they can also have a counter effect; particularly if there is a perception of favoritism involved, and can even lead to people changing the behavior in a negative way in order to achieve the reward. I once saw a department store sales manager sell an empty box (only contained packaging) to an unsuspecting customer because he was close to achieving his monthly sales target and cash bonus.

   I believe that a better approach is to demonstrate the value people bring through their efforts. To achieve this, make sure your request is clear and concise. Explain how the outcome will be used or be of benefit. If the request is likely to be a challenge for the person, then acknowledge that and let the person know you are confident in their abilities.

   Whilst the person is working on your request, make sure that you keep in touch with them, and provide positive feedback as frequently as possible. This is your opportunity to ensure they are not only on track but that you will get the outcome you were expecting. Communication is a two-way street so make sure you listen to any issues, risks and concerns raised by the person and take appropriate action to resolve them.

When the task is completed, acknowledge their efforts. If you are able, show them how the result they have produced has made a difference.

Showing appreciation to someone is really born out of respect for them as a human being. By demonstrating the value their efforts bring, they will be happier, and more likely to want to help you again in the future.

Engagement - Branding your vision

Part of the process of convincing your organisation to invest money and resources into your project involves selling it. In my experience, if you treat your project as though it was a product and then put together a catchy name or slogan then you'll have a much greater chance of success. The brand itself consists of an image, word or description that makes your project standout. Try and include one or two of your organisational values or principles in the brand or description as that demonstrates how your project fits in with the overall organisational direction. A word of caution – once you've branded your project and begin communicating that brand you may find it very challenging to change so take the time to create something meaningful and lasting, Test your brand with one or two key stakeholders and gauge their reactions. If they pick up on the brand quickly then you know you have a winner.

Branding tips

	Do
i.	Create a brand that supports your vision. Try and visualise how things might be when your project has been implemented.

	What does it look like? What does it feel like?
ii.	Keep it simple – one or two words ideally.
iii.	Tie your brand into your organisational vision.
iv.	Test your brand on a couple of people and gauge their reactions.
v.	Use your brand consistently in your communication as though the product already exists. Instead of saying "we have this project called Project X that will deliver ..." say "Project X will deliver ...".

	Don't
i.	Use acronyms. There are so many acronyms used in organisational conversations now without asking people to remember another one.
ii.	Try and come up with something for external use. Remember – the purpose of the brand is to help sell your project internally, not for convincing outside customers to buy it (although this does happen if you look at some of the large software companies and how they brand their products).

By way of example, I worked for a stockbroker once, and colleagues and I wanted to pursue developing a client advisor desktop system. There was an existing solution that, while functional, had significant performance issues that made uptake of the system poor. Literally it was the system that everyone loved to hate.

We established the vision for the new system, and identified the technical architecture for the development of the new solution. We knew it would be developed in the Java programming language, and we wanted give users the feeling of fun. We held a brain storming session to come up with some names:

"Java -> Coffee -> Caribbean -> Jamaica -> Fun ->Calypso music"

Thus the name we came up was *Calypso*. By the time we pitched the concept to Executive Management they were also calling it Calypso.

Two years after the solution had gone live, we asked the users if they wanted to change the name and there was an overwhelming response not to change it. Calypso had delivered on a promise, and the users had bought into it "as a product" so significantly that they wanted to drive future enhancements.

Chapter summary

Getting the solution right requires getting the right people with the right knowledge, skills and experience and utilising an effective leadership model to ensure that everyone involved feels as though they own the solution and want to see a successful outcome.

FRAMEWORKS

Below is just a small list of the kinds of resources available. Some of these have free content, and some you will have to purchase for use.

Agile Manifesto	<http://agilemanifesto.org>
Australian Privacy Laws	<http://www.oaic.gov.au/privacy/privacy-act/the-privacy-act>
Big Data Statistics	<http://wikibon.org/blog/big-data-statistics/>
Business Process Modeling and Notation (BPMN)	<http://www.bpmn.org>
DAMA International	< http://www.dama.org>
Data Governance Institute	<http://datagovernance.com>
Gartner IT Glossary	<http://www.gartner.com/it-glossary/>

HIPAA Privacy Rule	<http://www.hhs.gov/ocr/privacy/hipaa/administrative/privacyrule/>
IAIDQ	< http://iaidq.org>
ISO 29119 International Software Testing Standard	< http://softwaretestingstandard.org>
ISO 27001 Information Security Management	<http://www.iso.org/iso/home/standards/management-standards/iso27001.htm>
ISO 9000 – Quality Management	<http://www.iso.org/iso/home/standards/management-standards/iso_9000.htm>
ISO 9001 – Quality Management Principles	<http://www.iso.org/iso/qmp_2012.pdf>
ITIL	<http://www.itil-officialsite.com>
John Owens International	<http://jo-international.com/>
Mike 2.0	<http://mike2.openmethodology.org>
OData – Open Data Protocol	<http://www.odata.org>
The Data Warehouse Institute (TDWI)	<http://tdwi.org/Home.aspx>
The Open Data Handbook	<http://opendatahandbook.org/en/>
The Open Group Architecture Framework (TOGAF)	<http://www.theopengroup.org>
The Zachman Architecture Framework	<http://www.zachman.com/>
Trisotech Inc.	<http://www.trisotech.com>

BIBLIOGRAPHY

Books

Derby, Esther, and Diana Larsen. *Agile Retrospectives – Making Good Teams Great*, Dallas Texas: Pragmatic Bookshelf, 2008.

Kerth, Norman. *Project Retrospectives: A Handbook for Team Reviews*, New York: Dorset House Publishing, 2001.

Looi, Kelvin. *MDM for Customer Data*, Texas: MC Press Online LP, 2009.

Manns, Mary Lynn, and Linda Rising. *Fearless Change - Patterns for Introducing New Ideas*, Boston: Addison-Wesley, 2005.

Schmuller, Jospeh. *Teach Yourself UML in 24 Hours*, Indiana: Sams Publishing, 2004.

Spewak, Steven H. and Steven C. Hill. *Enterprise Architecture Planning*, New York: John Wiley & Sons, 1992.

Internet Resources

Anupindi, Nagesh V. "Inmon vs. Kimball - An Analysis", *Nagesh.com*, 25 Aug 2005, 27 Apr 2014, <http://www.nagesh.com/publications/technology/173-inmon-vs-kimball-an-analysis.html>.

Clear, James. "This Coach Improved Every Tiny Thing by 1 Percent and Here's What Happened", *JamesClear.com*, Jan 6 2014, 10 May 2014, <http://jamesclear.com/marginal-gains>.

"High Availability", *Wikipedia*, 25 Mar 2014, 14 Apr 2014, < http://en.wikipedia.org/wiki/High_availability>.

Hong, Kaylene. "China's Xiaomi sells 100,000 units of new $130 phone in 90 seconds, chalks up 7.45m reservations", *TheNextWeb.com*, 12 Aug 2013, 19 Apr 2014, <http://thenextweb.com/asia/2013/08/12/chinas-xiaomi-sells-100000-units-of-new-130-phone-in-90-seconds-chalks-up-7-45m-reservations/>.

McEwan, Scott. "Requirements – An Introduction", *IBM Developer Works*, 16 Apr 2004, 14 Apr 2014, <http://www.ibm.com/developerworks/rational/library/4166.html>.

Owens, John. "There Are No Such Things as Data Rules!" *John Owens Integrated Modeling Method*, 13 Oct 2010, 9 Apr 2014. <http://integrated-modeling-method.com/no-such-thing-as-data-rule/>.

Merrett, Rebecca. "How pizza businesses are using predictive analytics to optimize promotions", CIO.com, 7 Apr 2015, 10 Apr 2015, < http://www.cio.com.au/article/571920/how-pizza-businesses-using-predictive-analytics-optimise-promotions/?fp=16&fpid=1 >.

"PCI Data Security Standards", *PCI Security Standards Council*, 2006, 22 Jan 2015, < https://www.pcisecuritystandards.org/security_standards/>.

"PDCA: The Plan-Do-Check-Act Cycle", *Wikipedia*, 9 Apr 2014, 14 Apr 2014, <http://en.wikipedia.org/wiki/PDCA>.

Stamford, Conn. "Gartner says beware of the Data Lake fallacy",

Gartner.com, 28 Jul 2014, 4 Feb 2015, <http://www.gartner.com/newsroom/id/2809117>.

Stampler, Laura. "How Posting a Facebook Picture Saved a 3 Year Old's Sight", *Time.com*, 3 Apr 2014, 18 Apr 2014, <http://time.com/48216/facebook-picture-diagnoses-child-disease/>.

Van Der Meer, Erin. "Going, going, gone! Kate's £292 Diane Von Furstenberg dress sells out in just EIGHT MINUTES", *Daily Mail UK*, 17 Apr 2014, 18 Apr 2014, <http://www.dailymail.co.uk/femail/article-2606617/Kates-bold-patterned-dress-day-two-Australian-tour-sells-online-just-EIGHT-MINUTES.html>.

ABOUT THE AUTHOR

Shane is a dedicated and outcome focused Information Technology and business professional with an extensive track record of achieving business outcomes.

Recognised for significant contributions to a variety of organisations over a career spanning 20+ years, including land information management, banking and insurance, finance and wealth management, retail, manufacturing, and healthcare.

Shane possesses a Bachelor Applied Science (Computing) degree from QUT Brisbane Australia, and a number of industry certifications including TOGAF.

Shane is married with 4 children, and lives in Brisbane, Australia. #onedata

www.ingramcontent.com/pod-product-compliance
Lightning Source LLC
Chambersburg PA
CBHW041142050326
40689CB00001B/445